TEACHER'S GUIDE

STECK-VAUGHN

American Government

Freedom, Rights, Responsibilities

Vivian Bernstein

ISBN 0-8172-6344-6

6 7 8 RP 00 01

STECK-VAUGHN
ELEMENTARY · SECONDARY · ADULT · LIBRARY

A Harcourt Company

www.steck-vaughn.com

Table of Contents

About the Program

The democratic government of the United States has a tradition of being responsive to the voice of the people. The government exists for the people and by the people, who as citizens, participate in it. An understanding of the principles and structures of government is required for students to participate actively. Yet because many students throughout the nation have difficulty reading, they are unable to develop an adequate understanding of American government. The high reading levels found in basal government textbooks are an obstacle to these readers. They are frequently discouraged and bored. There has been a lack of interesting material about American government on a lower reading level. *American Government: Freedom, Rights, Responsibilities* provides these students with a stimulating program that prepares them for the challenges and responsibilities of being a citizen.

Organization of the Worktext

American Government is a course on government in the United States that covers how the Constitution was written; the principles and philosophies of the Constitution and the Bill of Rights; the structure of federal, state, and local governments; and the actions government takes to serve the American people.

American Government has been organized into five units. Each unit begins with an introduction that provides background information for understanding the unit and stimulates curiosity about the content of the unit. Each unit includes a biography about an outstanding American whose work relates to the themes of the unit. The **Focus on Government**, a primary-source document integral to the content, concludes each unit. Students have an opportunity to develop skills in reading original documents and to apply comprehension skills through written self-expression.

American Government, written on a fourth-to-fifth grade level, covers the high school government curriculum. The book has a high interest level that makes it appealing to middle school, high school, and adult students. Special features have been incorporated to make this program suitable for students with reading and learning difficulties. Questions at the beginning of each unit and chapter lead students in their reading. New social studies vocabulary is introduced in bold print and defined in the margins. The number of new vocabulary words is limited in each chapter, and most vocabulary words are reviewed and reused throughout the book. A total vocabulary list is included at the end of the book. The content load of facts and concepts is also controlled in each chapter. Photographs, graphs, and charts enhance the text.

A variety of activities that are designed to ensure comprehension and improve thinking and writing skills follows each chapter.

■ **Comprehension** activities enable students to improve their comprehension and recall skills while they test their knowledge of government information.

■ **Critical Thinking** activities are designed to develop essential critical thinking skills. Drawing conclusions, understanding cause and effect, differentiating between fact and opinion, identifying relevant information, and categorizing are some of the skills that are presented in the book. Students are taught each skill and then are given ample opportunity for practice.

■ **Skill Builder** activities are provided throughout the program, two per unit. This social studies skills program enables students to develop the skills they need to understand charts, political cartoons, and various types of graphs. The skill lessons build upon and reinforce factual information from the chapters.

Organization of the Teacher's Guide

The Teacher's Guide has been designed to enhance the activities of the worktext. The *Unit Teaching Strategies* offer unit-by-unit guidelines for the teacher.

■ **Concepts** set out the main ideas covered in this unit.

■ **Pre-Reading Activities** offer a variety of activities to develop concepts and background information before reading the unit. These activities prepare students for successful comprehension of the unit.

■ **Post-Reading Activities** offer a variety of activities that review and extend the content of each unit.

■ **Skill Builder** provides suggestions for using the two skill lessons in the unit.

■ **Focus on Government** offers strategies for teaching the primary-source material at the conclusion of each unit.

■ **People in Government** provides additional information about the person featured in the student text, discussion questions, and extension activities.

The *Chapter Teaching Strategies* provide chapter-by-chapter guidelines for the teacher.

■ **Objective** sets out the learning objectives for students.

■ **New Vocabulary** are all the new vocabulary words introduced in the chapter.

■ **Vocabulary Activities** offer creative opportunities for vocabulary building, which should follow introduction of the vocabulary.

■ **Reading Words** list potentially difficult reading words in the chapter.

■ **Review Words** are words that were new vocabulary in previous chapters, are reused in the current chapter, and should be reviewed before students read the new chapter.

■ **Pre-Reading Activities** set the stage for successful reading and comprehension.

■ **Post-Reading Activities** are activities to review and extend each chapter.

■ **Discussion Questions** provide comprehension and higher-level questions for small groups or whole-class discussions.

Four types of **Blackline Masters** are provided for teacher use.

■ **Graphic Organizers** help students summarize, organize, and apply critical thinking skills to information they are learning.

■ **Citizenship Activities** promote participation skills in government. These five activities extend the content of the text.

■ **Review Activities** cover key concepts and facts. There is one activity for each unit and one for the whole book.

■ **Tests** cover each of the five units and the entire book. The tests are designed to encourage student success.

General Teaching Suggestions

Teachers are encouraged to use the following suggestions where appropriate to their classroom situation and their students' needs. It should be recognized that students will proceed through the program according to their abilities and that the suggestions should be implemented accordingly.

1. Begin each unit by having students examine the Unit Opener. Discuss possible answers for the questions on the second page of each opener. Then refer to the *Unit Teaching Strategies* for introductory activities.

2. Begin each chapter with the **Pre-Reading Activities** found in the *Chapter Teaching Strategies*. Review the vocabulary words from previous chapters and introduce the new vocabulary. Encourage students to use the margin definitions for the new words. Suggestions for vocabulary introduction are found in the *Chapter Teaching Strategies*. Introduce words listed under **Reading Words** with which students may be unfamiliar.

3. Assist students as they read the chapter text. You may wish to have students read the text aloud. Point out how the photographs add to the text. Encourage students to refer to the charts and graphs.

4. Discuss the text with the students to reinforce facts and concepts. Discussion questions are included in the *Chapter Teaching Strategies*.

5. Students should complete the **Comprehension** activities independently when possible. Sometimes, a second reading of the text is helpful. When students cannot recall answers from memory, they should be encouraged to find the answers in the text.

6. Present new **Critical Thinking** activities to the class in brief group lessons. When possible, ask students to develop additional examples of the skill being taught by using information from previous chapters. Use the **Graphic Organizers** to extend the critical thinking lessons.

7. Present new **Skill Builder** activities to the class in brief group lessons. Encourage students to make their own charts and graphs when possible.

8. Discuss each writing activity with the class before students begin to write. Encourage students to use process writing techniques. Pre-writing, writing, peer sharing, and revising promote excellent writing.

9. Encourage writing by having students keep a social studies journal. Allow five minutes a day for students to summarize or respond in journal notebooks to their learning.

10. Blackline masters for review activities and tests should be completed at appropriate points during the course.

11. Help students work in the library to find biographies about government leaders. Encourage students to read about American history and understand how our government has changed since 1776.

12. Encourage students to write to government leaders and agencies to express their opinions or request information. A list of useful addresses is included in this guide on page 23.

13. Encourage students to follow news events and apply their knowledge of government for a better understanding of current events.

14. Whenever possible, organize field trips and invite guest speakers to introduce students to government institutions and leaders. These experiences will reinforce student knowledge about the government of the United States.

Teaching Strategies
UNIT 1 *Government for a New Nation*

Concepts:
- The Framers were influenced by concepts of democracy, representative government, and natural rights.
- The Framers borrowed these concepts from ancient Greece and Rome and from Great Britain.
- The Constitution included the principles of natural rights, popular sovereignty, limited government, separation of powers, and checks and balances.

Pre-Reading Activities: 1. Have students read the unit opener on pages 6 and 7. Ask students to identify the main ideas of Unit One. Discuss possible answers to the questions on page 7. **2.** Help students create a "What I Know" chart by dividing a paper into three columns with these headings: What I Know, Questions I Have, and What I Learned. Students should fill in the first two columns regarding how American government was formed. **3.** Locate on a world map: Great Britain; Athens, Greece; Rome, Italy; the United States. On a map of the United States, locate the Atlantic Ocean and the thirteen colonies.

Post-Reading Activities: 1. Divide the class into cooperative learning groups to study the Framers of the Constitution. Each group should research one Framer and present a report to the class. **2.** Have students complete the remaining column of the "What I Know" chart. **3.** Have the class form a Constitutional Convention to write a class constitution.

Skill Builder: 1. Review the steps in reading a line graph. After completing the Skill Builder on page 32, ask students to make line graphs that compare congressional representation for two states since 1950. Use the latest *World Almanac* to obtain statistics. **2.** Before having students complete the Skill Builder on page 41, ask students to name situations in which we obtain information from charts and tables.

People in Government: Madison had great influence on the development of the Constitution. He was later a member of Congress, a secretary of state, and as fourth President of the United States, he led the nation during the War of 1812. Most of what we know about the secret meetings of the Constitutional Convention comes from the journals Madison kept during the Convention. After reading the biography, have students write a paragraph summarizing Madison's contributions to the Constitution.

Focus on Government: Have various students participate in reading aloud this great speech. Acquire a recording of King making this speech, and share it with the students.

Chapter 1

Building a New Nation

Objective: Students will learn: The governments of ancient Athens and Rome and of Great Britain influenced the development of democratic government in the United States.

New Vocabulary: government, democracy, represent, representatives, trial, jury, peers, Parliament, prime minister

Vocabulary Activities: 1. Read and discuss with the students the margin definitions of the chapter's vocabulary. **2.** Have students use each word in oral sentences. **3.** Have students make two columns on a sheet of paper. Title one column Fair Trial and the other Parliamentary Government. List as many vocabulary words as possible under the appropriate headings.

Reading Words: lawmakers, Athens, Greece, citizens, population, Magna Carta, representative government, nobles, Great Britain, European, House of Lords, House of Commons, Constitution, Romans

Pre-Reading Activities: 1. Review with the class the causes of the American Revolution. **2.** Discuss the concept expressed by Lincoln's phrase "government of, by, and for the people." **3.** Discuss how the photograph on page 8 shows the influence of government on our daily lives. **4.** Examine the drawings on pages 9, 10, and 11. Discuss what each drawing shows about earlier governments. **5.** Define *Constitution*. Discuss how a constitution differs from laws.

Post-Reading Activities: 1. Use the Graphic Organizer blackline master on page 30 to develop ideas related to parliamentary government. Have students write the words *parliamentary government* inside the circle and ideas that relate to this form of government on the lines around the circle. **2.** Create a mock jury trial in which the teacher is accused of a hypothetical crime. **3.** Ask students to make a list of the advantages of democratic and representative governments.

Discussion Questions: 1. Why do we need government? How do you think government affects our daily lives? **2.** Why could direct democracy work in Athens but not as a government for the United States? **3.** How does representative government differ from direct democracy? **4.** How did the Magna Carta change British government? **5.** What ideas about government did Americans learn from Greece and Rome? **6.** How did the English Bill of Rights help the development of parliamentary government?

Chapter 2

Early Governments in the United States

Objective: Students will learn: The early colonial governments, the American fight for independence, and the Articles of Confederation influenced the development of the United States Constitution.

New Vocabulary: colonists, legislature, executive, governor, natural rights, liberty, delegates, independent, ratified

Vocabulary Activities: 1. Use the Graphic Organizer blackline master on page 30 to write down all new words associated with colonial governments. **2.** Have students use each of the vocabulary words in oral sentences.

Reading Words: colonies, elections, North America, France, Boston Harbor, First Continental Congress, Second Continental Congress, Declaration of Independence, Thomas Jefferson, Rhode Island, American Revolution, Articles of Confederation, central government

Review Words: representative, government, Parliament, democracy, jury, trial

Pre-Reading Activities: 1. Ask students to examine the chapter subtitles and photographs. Ask students to predict the contents of the chapter. **2.** Have students brainstorm why the people who lived in the colonies before 1776 might want to be independent from Great Britain. List reasons on the board. **3.** Ask students to imagine being at the Second Continental Congress. Ask: What laws would you write for the new nation? Discuss the challenges of creating fair, effective laws.

Post-Reading Activities: 1. Have the class create a flow chart to show the sequence of events from 1753 to 1787. Survey the chapter for dates and events to add to the chart. **2.** Read the Declaration of Independence on pages 204–208 and discuss its meaning. What ideas in the Declaration of Independence should be used in planning the government for the new nation? **3.** Divide the class into cooperative learning groups. Assign each group a different colony. Have them research the government of that colony and report to the class on their findings.

Discussion Questions: 1. How did the colonial governments help Americans learn about representative government? **2.** What ideas about democracy and representative government did the colonists borrow from Great Britain? **3.** Do you think British laws were unfair to the colonists? Which laws? Why? **4.** What were the weaknesses of the Articles of Confederation?

Chapter 3

Writing the Constitution

Objective: Students will learn: The Framers followed major principles and reached important compromises when they wrote the Constitution.

New Vocabulary: popular sovereignty, separation of powers, legislative, judicial, checks and balances, federalism, compromise, senators, amendments, ratification, majority

Vocabulary Activities: 1. Explain the pronunciation and meaning of each word. Ask students for examples of sentences that show how each vocabulary word can be used. **2.** Explain that *compromise* is used both as a noun and a verb. *Legislative* and *judicial* are adjectives.

Reading Words: laws of the land, Framers, Constitutional Convention, secrecy, limited government, organized, population, representation, landowners, federal government, agreement, slavery, Congress, Senate

Review Words: delegates, representatives, democracy, government, natural rights, liberty, ratified

Pre-Reading Activities: 1. Divide students into cooperative learning groups to create lists of ten items that could be included in the plans for a democratic government. Have each group present its list to the class. **2.** List on the board the six principles agreed on by all of the Framers. Discuss their meaning and how they promote democracy. **3.** The Constitution was the result of several compromises. Ask students to give examples of how compromises are needed in their own lives. **4.** In a democracy, the majority rules. Discuss why this is fair or unfair.

Post-Reading Activities: 1. Have students use the Graphic Organizer blackline master on page 29 to compare the Articles of Confederation with the Constitution. **2.** Have students write a paragraph that explains one of the important compromises of the Constitution. **3.** Have students work in pairs to make a chart that compares the government created by the Framers with the parliamentary government of Great Britain.

Discussion Questions: 1. Why did the Framers decide to replace the Articles of Confederation with the Constitution? **2.** Why did the Framers decide to hold all Convention meetings secretly? **3.** Why did the Framers want a separation of powers and checks and balances? **4.** What were the Three-Fifths Compromise and the Great Compromise? Do you think these compromises were good for the nation? Why or why not? **5.** If you lived in 1787, would you vote for or against ratification? Explain why.

Chapter 4

Understanding Our Constitution

Objective: Students will learn: The Constitution was written to be a flexible document that would promote representative democracy through separation of powers and checks and balances.

New Vocabulary: Preamble, document, justice, articles, officials, commander in chief, declare war, veto, override, treaties, abuse, proposed

Vocabulary Activities: 1. Have the class organize vocabulary words in two columns under the headings Constitution and Three Branches of Government. **2.** Explain the meaning of each word. Then have students use each word in a sentence. **3.** Have students use the Graphic Organizer blackline master on page 30 to create a word web around the word *Constitution*.

Reading Words: democratic, enforce, advisers, constitutional, unconstitutional, appointments, commits, guidelines, elastic clause, flexibility

Review Words: natural rights, liberty, ratified, judicial, executive, checks and balances, separation of powers, compromise, amendments

Pre-Reading Activities: 1. Have students write five questions about the Constitution. Have them try to answer some of the questions before reading the chapter. **2.** Have the class try to answer the pre-reading questions on page 33. Encourage students to survey and skim the chapter to get information. **3.** Demonstrate the elastic quality of a rubber band. Discuss the term *elastic clause* and how it has allowed the Constitution to be a flexible document.

Post-Reading Activities: 1. Have students work in cooperative learning groups to develop lists of ten quiz questions about the chapter. Groups should exchange quizzes and try to answer the questions. **2.** Have students read and analyze the Preamble. Have them write a paragraph that tells the goals of the Constitution. **3.** Tell the class that the Constitution is the highest law of the land. Discuss what that means. **4.** Have students write a paragraph that explains three ways the Constitution protects freedom and liberty.

Discussion Questions: 1. What are some of the checks and balances in the Constitution? How do checks and balances protect our freedom? **2.** What is separation of powers, and what are three examples of the separation of powers? **3.** What does the phrase "We the People" from the Preamble mean? **4.** How does the Constitution limit the power of the President? Is it important for the President's power to be limited? Why or why not?

Chapter 5

The Bill of Rights and Other Amendments

Objective: Students will learn: The Bill of Rights was written because many states wanted the rights of every American to be guaranteed. Seventeen other amendments have been added to the Constitution.

New Vocabulary: guarantee, assembly, civil rights, petition, due process, guilty, double jeopardy, naturalized, suffrage, terms

Vocabulary Activities: 1. Read, pronounce, and explain the meaning of each word. **2.** Have students locate the sentences and definitions that introduce the words *double jeopardy*, *due process*, *naturalized*, *suffrage*, and *terms* in the text. Have students write their own sentences using those words. **3.** Write *Guarantee*, *Assembly*, *Civil Rights*, and *Petition* as headings on the board. Ask students to provide examples for each word.

Reading Words: disagreed, Bill of Rights, freedom of religion, freedom of the press, freedom of speech, freedom of assembly, separation of church and state, Vietnam, evidence, accused, equal rights, poll tax, Civil War, equal protection clause

Review Words: jury, trial, representatives, amendments, ratified, civil rights, senators

Pre-Reading Activities: 1. Ask students to skim the chapter and prepare six questions that ask who, what, when, where, why, and how about the chapter. Share the questions with the class, and see how many can be answered before reading. **2.** Explain each of the five freedoms of the First Amendment. Have students give reasons why those freedoms are important to democracy. **3.** Discuss the meanings of *due process* and *equal protection under the law*.

Post-Reading Activities: 1. Have students choose one of the five freedoms and write a paragraph telling why it is important. **2.** What constitutional rights did Martin Luther King, Jr., use when he led his March on Washington in 1963? What rights did he work for?

Discussion Questions: 1. Why did the Framers add the Bill of Rights to the Constitution? **2.** How does the "separation of church and state" clause of the First Amendment affect American life? **3.** Why have civil rights laws been passed by Congress? **4.** Do you agree with the Twenty-sixth Amendment that allows eighteen-year-olds to vote? Do you think the voting age should be raised or lowered? Tell why. **5.** Do you agree with the Twenty-second Amendment, which limits the President to two terms in office? Tell why.

Note: A review activity covering Unit 1 is provided on pages 32-33 of this guide. A test covering Unit 1 is provided on page 34.

UNIT 2 *Three Branches of the Federal Government*

Concepts:
- Congress has many powers, but its main job is lawmaking.
- The President represents the United States in a variety of roles.
- The laws of Congress are carried out by the President and the huge executive bureaucracy.
- The Supreme Court has the power of judicial review.
- Many steps are needed for a bill to become a law.

Pre-Reading Activities: 1. Read and discuss the Unit Opener on pages 52-53. Have students brainstorm possible answers to the questions on page 53. **2.** Review with the class the information they have learned about the federal government in Unit 1. **3.** Have students create a "What I Know" chart. (See Pre- Reading Activities for Unit 1.) Have students complete the first two columns with facts about the federal government.

Post-Reading Activities: 1. Have students use the Graphic Organizer blackline master on page 31 of this guide to show the features of the three branches of the federal government. Have students write *federal government* in the large box and the names of the three branches in the boxes below. In the remaining boxes, have students list features of each branch. **2.** Have students complete the remaining column of the "What I Know" chart. **3.** Have students write a paragraph explaining the role of one of the three branches of government. **4.** Help students use a *World Almanac* to learn about recent actions of each branch of government.

Skill Builder: 1. Help students interpret the political cartoon on page 71. After they have completed the Skill Builder, have students find a political cartoon in a newspaper and write two or three sentences explaining the cartoon. **2.** Review the steps in reading a bar graph. Help students complete the Skill Builder. Have students work in pairs to make bar graphs that compare the political party affiliations of members of the House of Representatives for three states. Use the *World Almanac* for information.

People in Government: As a Texas senator, Barbara Jordan worked for civil rights and laws for farmers. She served on the House Judiciary Committee that investigated Watergate, and she was the keynote speaker at the 1976 Democratic National Convention. In 1978 she became a professor at the University of Texas. Have students research another minority member of Congress and present a brief biography to the class.

Focus on Government: Ask students to discuss the many ways the *Brown v. Board of Education* decision affected integration. Ask students to consider the risks taken by Linda Brown.

Chapter 6

Congress: The Lawmaking Branch

Objective: Students will learn: Congress has the constitutional power to write laws, add amendments, and carry out various other jobs. Congress is organized into two houses.

New Vocabulary: oath, immigration, copyrights, patents, committee, political party, census, *pro tempore*, adjourns

Vocabulary Activities: 1. Discuss the meaning of each word. Have students use the words in oral sentences. **2.** Have students use the Graphic Organizer blackline master on page 30 of this guide to create a word web around *political party*. **3.** Discuss where copyright and patent information can be found on products. Why are copyrights and patents issued?

Reading Words: marriage, divorce, organized, familiar, major, district, reelected, population, requirements, in common, graduated, Hispanic, minority party, racial, appoint, session, extremely

Review Words: abuse, proposed, senator, representative, term

Pre-Reading Activities: 1. Review with the class the facts that were learned about Congress in Unit 1. **2.** Have students brainstorm possible answers to the pre-reading questions on page 54. **3.** Ask students to examine the chart on page 55. Discuss the meaning of each power. Ask: How do these powers affect our lives? **4.** Have students brainstorm qualities that members of Congress should have.

Post-Reading Activities: 1. Have students use the Graphic Organizer blackline master on page 30 to show the powers of Congress. **2.** Have students write a paragraph that explains the limits of Congress' power. They should include at least four things Congress cannot do. **3.** For one week, have students check the newspaper daily to find out about current actions by Congress. At the end of the week, have students choose one story and report on it to the class. **4.** Have students complete the Citizenship Activity 1 blackline master on page 24 to create a profile of a senator or representative. Then have the students write to that senator or representative for more information. **5.** Have students write to the United States patent office for information about obtaining a patent. **6.** Invite a postal service worker to talk to the class about the postal service and how it carries out its job.

Discussion Questions: 1. Why does Congress do most of its work in committees? **2.** Why can the number of representatives a state sends to the House of Representatives change? **3.** Do you think a census every ten years is necessary? Tell why. **4.** Explain why Congress is the voice of the American people. **5.** Why must Congress sometimes pass laws Americans dislike?

Chapter 7

The President and the Executive Branch

Objective: Students will learn: The President is the leader of the executive branch and has a variety of responsibilities and powers. The Vice President is the leader of the Senate and will become President if that person is suddenly incapacitated.

New Vocabulary: execute, presidency, image, responsibilities, agencies, budget, policies, Chief of State, symbol, ambassadors, opposes, impeach, pardoned, bureaus, bureaucracy

Vocabulary Activities: 1. Have students create two lists, one titled The President Works For Us and the other titled The President Stands For Us. Have them put as many new words under each list as they can. **2.** Ask students to use the words in oral sentences that illustrate their meaning. **3.** Have students use the Graphic Organizer blackline master on page 30 to create a vocabulary word web with *President's Responsibilities* in the middle.

Reading Words: solemnly, faithfully, Christian, John F. Kennedy, chief diplomat, Watergate Scandal, Richard Nixon, campaign, "cover up", resigned, committed

Review Words: oath, governor, political party, checks and balances, override, veto, guilty, committee

Pre-Reading Activities: 1. Ask students to review what they remember from Unit 1 about the executive branch. List facts on the board. **2.** Have the class read the first and last paragraphs and survey the photographs, captions, and subtitles. Ask the class to predict what they will learn from the chapter. **3.** Ask students to work in pairs to list what they think are the most important qualities a President should have. Have students share their answers.

Post-Reading Activities: 1. Divide the class into cooperative learning groups to create charts listing the six jobs of a President. Include examples of how the President carries out each job. **2.** Have students write to the President about an issue they believe is important. Review the format of a business letter. **3.** Have students use a library book to learn about one of the United States Presidents. Prepare brief reports that include important achievements. **4.** Have students follow for a week a news story that involves the President. Have them summarize the President's activities and group them according to his six jobs.

Discussion Questions: 1. Why does a President need the right image? **2.** Compare the roles of Vice President and President. **3.** Why is it important for a Vice President to immediately become President if the President dies? What laws in the Constitution require this? **4.** What are some powers the President does not have? **5.** Do you agree with President Ford's decision to pardon Richard Nixon? Explain why.

Chapter 8

The Executive Branch at Work

Objective: Students will learn: Hundreds of agencies and millions of workers are needed to enforce the laws of Congress.

New Vocabulary: national security, annual, secretary, inspects, low income, coining, counterfeit, undocumented, civil service

Vocabulary Activities: 1. Have students derive other words using *inspect* as the root word. **2.** Have students find the root word of both parts of *national security*. Have them write a definition for that term using what they know about the root meanings. **3.** Have students find the meanings for the two parts of *low income* and *civil service*. Then have them draw conclusions about what the terms mean. **4.** Explain that *secretary* does not refer to an office worker, but rather to a leader of a Cabinet department.

Reading Words: department, staff, policies, organize, National Security Council, Office of Management and Budget, labor, agriculture, inspector, treasury, President McKinley, legal, research

Review Words: agencies, bureaucracy, independent, budget, civil rights, immigration, responsibilities, executive

Pre-Reading Activities: 1. Have students brainstorm reasons for the existence of a huge executive bureaucracy. **2.** Survey the subtitles and five pages of charts. Ask students to name some of the many federal agencies listed on the charts and to describe their purpose. **3.** Discuss the many places where we come in contact with civil service workers at all levels of government.

Post-Reading Activities: 1. Have students create a chart that shows how the executive branch is organized into the Executive Office, executive departments, and independent agencies. Students should list the various leaders, agencies, and departments that belong in each category. **2.** Have students use the Graphic Organizer blackline master on page 31 to show the executive department. Have students write *An Executive Department* in the large box. Write the names of three agencies that belong to that department in the three boxes beneath the large box. In the boxes below that, write one goal for each agency.

Discussion Questions: 1. Which people in the executive bureaucracy work closely with the President? **2.** Why does the President need a Cabinet and a White House staff? **3.** Why are some federal workers appointed by the President while most are civil service workers? **4.** Explain how some departments and agencies help the nation.

Chapter 9

Justice for All: The Judicial Branch

Objective: Students will learn: Congress set up three types of federal courts. Supreme Court decisions have a lasting impact on the nation.

New Vocabulary: appealed, overturn, precedents, judicial review, segregation, desegregation

Vocabulary Activities: 1. Introduce the meaning of the prefix *de-*. After defining *segregate* have students work out the meanings of *segregation* and *desegregation*. **2.** Have students locate the sentences where the words are introduced in the text. Have them read the definitions, read the sentences with the vocabulary words, and then write independent sentences using each word.

Reading Words: establish, District Courts, approval, Courts of Appeals, requirement, justices, publish, constitutional, unconstitutional, reverse, *Plessy v. Ferguson*, *Brown v. Topeka Board of Education*, interpret, interpretation

Review Words: justice, trial, jury, majority, due process, civil rights

Pre-Reading Activities: 1. Review what students learned in Unit 1 about the Supreme Court, due process, the Fourteenth Amendment, and civil rights. **2.** Review the role of the judicial branch in the system of checks and balances. **3.** Discuss the phrase "equal justice for all." Ask: What does it mean? Why do we need a court system to have justice?

Post-Reading Activities: 1. Have students use the Graphic Organizer blackline master on page 31 to depict the federal court system. Students should write *The Federal Court System* in the large box. The three types of courts should be placed in the three boxes below. Under that, they should briefly write the purpose of each court. **2.** Have students use the library to write a brief biography of one of the current Supreme Court justices. Have students share their reports. **3.** Divide the class into cooperative learning groups to learn about an important Supreme Court case and how it has influenced American life. Some suggested cases are: *Muller v. Oregon*, *Roth v. U.S.*, *Mapp v. Ohio*, *Regents of Univ. of Calif. v. Bakke*, *Engel v. Vitale*, *Miranda v. Arizona*, and *Gideon v. Wainwright*.

Discussion Questions: 1. What kinds of cases are heard in each type of federal court? **2.** Do you agree that all federal judges should be appointed by the President? Why or why not? **3.** What are the four kinds of decisions the Supreme Court makes? Give examples. **4.** Why is judicial review an important power? **5.** How did *Brown v. Topeka Board of Education* affect segregation?

Chapter 10

How a Bill Becomes a Law

Objective: Students will learn: It takes many steps for a bill to pass through Congress and become a law. The President can use his veto power to prevent a bill from becoming law. Congress can overturn a President's veto.

New Vocabulary: subcommittee, debate, amends, filibusters, constituents, conference committee

Vocabulary Activities: 1. Define *committee* and *conference*. Introduce the prefix *sub-*. Have students write definitions for *subcommittee* and *conference committee*. **2.** Have students find synonyms for *debate*. **3.** Remind students of the previous vocabulary word *amendment*. Have them derive the meaning of *amend*.

Reading Words: commercials, process, veteran, membership, Strom Thurmond, assigned, pocket veto

Review Words: agencies, amendments, political party, senators, adjourns, veto, override, compromise

Pre-Reading Activities: 1. Review with the class what they have learned about lawmaking from the previous chapters. **2.** Discuss with the class the necessity for laws and the role of laws in a democracy. **3.** Have students list the many areas in their lives that are affected by laws. **4.** Have students brainstorm the importance of debate in the lawmaking process.

Post-Reading Activities: 1. Divide the class into cooperative learning groups to create a flow chart to illustrate the steps a bill must follow in order to become a law. **2.** Help students role-play the steps needed for a bill to become a law. Students should begin by proposing bills that would apply to their school. They should then form committees to consider those bills. **3.** Have students write a letter to a member of Congress, urging that member to support or oppose a bill currently under consideration. The letters should include one or two reasons for their point of view. **4.** Have students use the library to research one of the following: a recent presidential veto; a recent Congressional overturning of a veto; a recent law overturned by the Supreme Court; the voting record of a member of Congress.

Discussion Questions: 1. Most bills are never passed into law. Why? **2.** What do committees and subcommittees do with bills? **3.** Do you think the voting records of members of Congress should be made public? Tell why. **4.** What can Congress do after the President vetoes a bill? **5.** How does our lawmaking process encourage democracy?

Note: A review activity covering Unit 2 is provided on pages 35-36 of this guide. A test covering Unit 2 is provided on page 37.

UNIT 3 *State and Local Government*

Concepts:
- State governments were created by the Constitution; local governments are created by the states.
- State governments are based on limited government, separation of powers, and checks and balances.
- Local governments provide services to the people.
- It is easier for citizens to interact with state and local government than with the federal government.

Pre-Reading Activities: 1. Have students read the unit opener on pages 104-105. Discuss possible answers to the questions on page 105. **2.** Have students examine the photographs in Unit 3. Discuss what the photographs tell us about state and local governments. **3.** Review the major principles of the United States Constitution. Ask students how they think these ideas apply to state and local governments. **4.** Have students follow a local or state story in the newspaper for one week. Have them report to the class on that story and the government's involvement in it.

Post-Reading Activities: 1. Have students use the Graphic Organizer blackline master on page 31 to show how state governments are organized into three branches. They should write *State Government* in the top box, then below it the three branches, and below that the role of each branch. **2.** Have the class write letters to their state senators requesting information about state programs and laws for protecting the environment. **3.** Invite a local city council member, a police officer, sheriff, or other government officer to visit the class and discuss the role of local government.

Skill Builder: 1. Review the steps needed to read a bar graph. After students complete the Skill Builder, have them make bar graphs that compare the number of members in state legislatures for four states. Statistics can be obtained from an almanac. **2.** Review the skills needed for understanding circle graphs. After students complete the Skill Builder, help them make circle graphs that compare population age groups in several cities. Statistics can be obtained from an almanac.

People in Government: Harold Washington mobilized the African American population of Chicago to become voters. Have students work in pairs to learn about other minority mayors around the nation.

Focus on Government: Discuss the wide variety of topics that were on the agenda for the city council meeting. Ask students which items they believe were most important and why. Have students attend a local city council meeting and report on the proceedings.

Chapter 11

Federalism's Other Side

Objective: Students will learn: State governments try to meet the specific needs of each state in a variety of ways. State constitutions are both similar and different from the United States Constitution.

New Vocabulary: industry, integrate, environment

Vocabulary Activities: 1. Discuss the meaning of each word. Ask students to use the words in oral sentences. **2.** Create word webs for *industry* and *environment*.

Reading Words: contact, Alaska, Rhode Island, California, Florida, Oregon, Pennsylvania, interpret, original, inspection, professional, certificate, promote, denies, disabilities, graduation, pollution, recycling, impact

Review Words: separation of powers, segregation, checks and balances, amendments, popular sovereignty, legislative, executive, judicial, agencies, legislature, budget, treaties

Pre-Reading Activities: 1. Have students tell as many differences among the fifty states as they can. List the differences on the chalkboard. Help them conclude that different state governments are needed to meet these special needs and characteristics. **2.** Brainstorm with the class to predict answers to the pre-reading questions on page 106. **3.** Help students locate on a large map of the United States the states mentioned in the chapter. (States are listed under Reading Words.)

Post-Reading Activities: 1. Have students use the Graphic Organizer blackline master on page 29 to compare state and federal governments. Have them list the differences in the left and right sections and the common features in the middle section. **2.** Divide the class into cooperative learning groups and have them list all the ways they come in contact with state governments. Then have each group compare its list with that of the others. **3.** Have students write a letter to their governor, asking that he or she take action on a problem that is important to the students. Students should include at least two reasons for their point of view. **4.** Have students find out about their state's constitution. Is it the original? How many amendments have been added?

Discussion Questions: 1. Discuss the ways the fifty states differ from each other. **2.** Why does each state need its own laws? Give examples. **3.** How are state constitutions similar to and different from the United States Constitution? **4.** What powers belong to the states? To the federal government? To both? **5.** What do state education agencies do?

Chapter 12

State Governments at Work

Objective: Students will learn: The three branches of state government work together to serve the people.

New Vocabulary: apportioned, initiative, referendum, militia, sentences, convicted, civil, criminal

Vocabulary Activities: 1. Have students find the root words of *referendum* and *criminal*. **2.** Organize the words under two headings: Lawmaking and Trials. Group as many vocabulary words as possible under each heading.

Reading Words: mature, apply, districts, representation, assigned, approve, item veto, National Guard, riot, appointed, qualified, involved, graduate, argument, murder, intermediate, accused, general election, elderly, disabled, polluted, casino gambling, Montana, Massachusetts, Mississippi, New Jersey, Maryland, Chesapeake Bay

Review Words: proposed, debate, veto, governor, majority, policies, budgets, pardon, responsibilities, appeal, due process, industries

Pre-Reading Activities: 1. Review what the class learned about the role of the three branches of the federal government. Tell them that state governments also have three branches. **2.** Have students survey the chapter by reading the pre-reading questions and the subtitles. Have students write five questions that they expect to answer after they have read the text. List some of these questions on the board. **3.** Have students locate on a large United States map the states and places mentioned in the chapter (see Reading Words).

Post-Reading Activities: 1. Use the Graphic Organizer blackline master on page 30 to show the jobs and powers of a state governor. **2.** Have students write business letters to a state senator requesting information about a bill he or she is currently supporting. **3.** Divide the class into cooperative learning groups to list ways we interact with state government and how state laws affect our lives. Have them also list laws that might be different in a neighboring state. **4.** Invite a local judge to visit the class and discuss the state judicial system. **5.** Have students work in pairs to research two or three recent laws passed by their state legislature. Have the students present their research to the class.

Discussion Questions: 1. How is lawmaking by state government similar to lawmaking by the federal government? **2.** Discuss ways citizens can be involved in the lawmaking process in some state governments. **3.** Do you think being a governor is good experience for becoming President of the United States? Why or why not? **4.** What are the three types of state courts, and what roles do they play in the justice system?

Chapter 13

Thousands of Local Governments

Objective: Students will learn: There are several types of local governments and different methods of governing, but they all serve the communities.

New Vocabulary: counties, sheriff, district attorney, municipal, city charter

Vocabulary Activities: 1. As a class activity, create word webs around *county government* and *municipal government*. Use words from the text, as well as the margin vocabulary words, to complete the webs around each type of government.

Reading Words: collapsed, local, communities, utility, needy, mass-transit, create, rural, urban, ceremonies, manager, suburbs, Connecticut, Rhode Island, San Francisco, Los Angeles, California

Review Words: executive, budget, policies, low income, citizen, petition

Pre-Reading Activities: 1. Discuss the services that students receive from their local governments. Tell students they will be learning how different types of local governments provide services to the people. **2.** Have students locate on a United States map the states and cities mentioned in the chapter. (See Reading Words for names of states and cities.) **3.** Ask students to name some of the elected members of their local government. **4.** Have students find in the newspaper a news story about the local government. Have them briefly describe the story to the class.

Post-Reading Activities: 1. Have students describe the different ways county and city governments are organized. **2.** Have students create a list of laws for a model city charter. **3.** There are many opportunities for people to do volunteer work in their local communities. Have the class list community organizations that depend on volunteers. They may use the local phone book to help complete this list. Help students learn how they can become volunteers, what skills are needed, and the type of services volunteers perform. **4.** Invite a member of the local government to visit the class and discuss his or her responsibilities.

Discussion Questions: 1. Why do states create local governments? **2.** Do you think the Constitution should have listed the powers of local governments? **3.** What do you think is the best type of government for a city? Tell why. **4.** Discuss ways people can interact with their local government. **5.** When a city has a council-mayor plan of government, the manager is an executive who was not elected. Do you think this is a fair government for a democracy?

Note: A review activity covering Unit 3 is provided on page 38. A test covering Unit 3 is provided on page 39.

UNIT 4 *Democracy at Work*

Concepts:
• The campaign and election process is dominated by two major political parties.
• Nonvoting is a serious problem.
• It is a long, expensive process for candidates to enter primaries, win their party's nomination, and conduct presidential campaigns.
• Interest groups work hard to influence lawmaking in Congress.
• Interest groups form PACs to help candidates win elections.

Pre-Reading Activities: 1. Have students read and discuss the unit opener on pages 132 and 133. Ask students to brainstorm possible answers to the questions on page 133. **2.** Have students brainstorm why elections and efforts to influence government are part of a government "by the people." **3.** Have students use the Graphic Organizer blackline master on page 30 to show what they know about campaigns and elections. Have them write *Campaigns and Elections* in the middle.

Post-Reading Activities: 1. Have students read back issues of newspapers in the library to learn about a recent local or national election campaign. Then have students use the Graphic Organizer blackline master on page 29 to compare and contrast the platforms of the opposing candidates. **2.** Have students write paragraphs to persuade people to use their voting rights. **3.** Invite a local elected official to discuss with the class how he or she campaigned during the election.

Skill Builder: 1. Review the skills needed for reading circle graphs. After completing the Skill Builder, students should make two circle graphs that compare the percentages of Democrats to Republicans in Congress. One graph should be for the Senate and the other for the House of Representatives. Use an almanac for statistics. **2.** Review the skills needed for reading line graphs. Help students locate and read a line graph in the business section of a newspaper.

People in Government: Before becoming one of Ronald Reagan's speech writers, Peggy Noonan was a news writer for radio and television. Noonan's work helped influence citizens to vote for Bush. Acquire the text of a speech of Reagan or Bush and have students read it aloud. Discuss how Noonan used the language to persuade or influence the listeners.

Focus on Government: Discuss with students the variety of appearances Kassebaum made on her campaign tour. Ask: Why would she stop at these various places? How much time did Kassebaum have to herself? What kind of job would her campaign staff have had to do to make a tour like this possible?

Chapter 14

Political Parties and Voters

Objective: Students will learn: Political parties are an important component of American government. Voters must meet certain requirements; voter behavior can be described; a large number of potential voters choose not to vote, for a variety of reasons.

New Vocabulary: candidates, polling places, platform, registration

Vocabulary Activities: 1. Have students divide a sheet of paper into four columns. Use a vocabulary word as a heading for each column. Beneath the headings, list other words that are associated with the vocabulary words. **2.** Have students use the Graphic Organizer blackline master on page 30 to create a word web around the term *voting*.

Reading Words: Republicans, Democrats, advertising, competition, Federalists, Anti-Federalists, Libertarian Party, issues, environmental, requirement, North Dakota, qualified, disabilities, participate, cast their vote

Review Words: political party, oppose, ratification, represent, democracy, majority, naturalization, debates

Pre-Reading Activities: 1. Ask students to describe what they remember about the last presidential election: political parties, campaign activities, and voter behavior. **2.** Discuss the importance of voting in a democracy.

Post-Reading Activities: 1. Have students use the Graphic Organizer blackline master on page 30 to organize their ideas about nonvoting. Then have them use the word web to write paragraphs that explain why millions of people do not vote. **2.** Divide the class into cooperative learning groups to research various third parties. Suggestions include: Free Soil, Prohibition, Socialist Labor, "Bull Moose," Libertarian. **3.** Invite a member from the local branches of each major political party to visit the class. Ask the party members to discuss what makes their party unique from the others. **4.** Have students research why the elephant and donkey have come to be symbols of the Republican and Democratic parties.

Discussion Questions: 1. What are five ways political parties help the nation? **2.** How can third parties influence elections? **3.** Who are the nation's qualified voters? How do they register to vote? **4.** North Dakota does not require voter registration, but it has one of the highest voter turnouts in elections. Do you think other states should follow North Dakota's policy? Why or why not?

Chapter 15

Campaigns and Elections

Objective: Students will learn: The election process involves nominations, primaries, national conventions, and campaigns. Campaigns are expensive, and the sources of campaign funds are varied.

Vocabulary: ballot, nominate, primary elections, rallies, public funds, public opinion, propaganda, media

Vocabulary Activities: 1. Have students use the Graphic Organizer blackline master on page 30 to create a word web using vocabulary around the term *elections*. **2.** Have students use the definition of *public* to define *public funds* and *public opinion*.

Reading Words: process, convention, presidential, campaign, Michael Dukakis, advertising, commercial, advertisement, bumper stickers, expense, manager, fund-raising, taxpayer, influence, opponents, public opinion polls, voting booth

Review Words: candidate, delegates, political parties, image debates, polling places, registration

Pre-Reading Activities: 1. Have students survey the chapter by examining the subtitles, first and last paragraphs, and photographs. They should write five questions that they expect to answer after reading the chapter. Collect the questions and use them after the chapter reading. **2.** Discuss with the class the ways businesses use advertising to sell their products. Tell the students that similar methods are used by campaign managers. Ask: How could campaign managers best influence voters? **3.** Discuss with students the task facing presidential candidates in persuading a majority of voters to vote for them. Have students brainstorm methods candidates can use in reaching the voters.

Post-Reading Activities: 1. Divide the class into cooperative learning groups to make a flow chart illustrating the many steps in the election process. **2.** Have students complete the Citizenship Activity 2 blackline master on page 25. **3.** Have students learn more about voting and elections by reading a library book and writing a brief report. **4.** Have students complete the Citizenship Activity 3 blackline master on page 26.

Discussion Questions: 1. What must candidates do to win the presidential nomination of their political party? **2.** What happens at a national party convention? **3.** Why do candidates need large amounts of campaign money? **4.** How do candidates get campaign money? **5.** How do candidates try to influence public opinion?

Chapter 16

PACs and Interest Groups

Objective: Students will learn: There are several types of interest groups that try to influence elections and lawmaking. Congress limits the power of PACs and interest groups.

New Vocabulary: lobby, discrimination

Vocabulary Activity: 1. Discuss the political meaning of *lobby*. Ask students to extend the meaning to *lobbyists* and *lobbying*. **2.** Have students find examples of discrimination in their school or community.

Reading Words: organization, commercials, influenced, stricter, benefit, issues, activity, professional, medical, publishes, Chamber of Commerce, informed, lobbyists, advertisements, interview, contribute, source, development, discrimination, equal pay

Review Words: registration, media, proposed, committees, candidates, public opinion

Pre-Reading Activities: 1. Discuss with the class ways they could try to influence government. Conclude with the idea that by forming groups, people can work more effectively to influence government. **2.** Ask students to name some interest groups with which they are familiar. **3.** Brainstorm with students ways that legislators could be influenced. Write the students' ideas on the chalkboard. Discuss which of these ways could be considered illegal.

Post-Reading Activities: 1. Use the Graphic Organizer blackline master on page 31 to classify information about the three types of interest groups. Include at least one example of each. **2.** Have students make charts listing the positive and negative features of PACs and interest groups. **3.** Divide the class into cooperative learning groups to research a public interest group, such as the League of Women Voters or Common Cause. Encourage students to write to the interest group for information. How does the group try to serve all people in the nation? **4.** Invite a lobbyist from a local chapter of an interest group to discuss with the class the role of interest groups and the job of a lobbyist.

Discussion Questions: 1. How was Candy Lightner able to influence the government to pass laws against drunk drivers? **2.** Give examples of how some interest groups have helped the nation. How can they hurt the nation? **3.** How do professional lobbyists influence Congress? **4.** Do you think PACs should be allowed to run their own political campaigns? Why? **5.** Do you think PACs should be allowed to contribute as much money as they please to political campaigns? Why or why not?

Note: A review activity covering Unit 4 is provided on page 40 of this guide. A test covering Unit 4 is provided on page 41.

Unit 5   *Government in Action*

Concepts:
- Different kinds of taxes are needed to pay for government budgets.
- The police, justice system, and military branches protect the United States and its people.
- Other forms of democracy, like Sweden's parliamentary democracy, also protect freedom and liberty.
- Other forms of government, such as those of China and Saudi Arabia, are authoritarian and allow little personal freedom.
- American foreign policy is constantly changing to help the United States work with other nations.

Pre-Reading Activities: 1. Read and discuss the Unit Opener on pages 164-165. Help students brainstorm possible answers to the questions on page 165. **2.** Discuss with the class what they know about taxes, the federal budget, and foreign policy. **3.** Brainstorm with the class ways the government can protect the people and national security.

Post-Reading Activities: 1. Have students complete the Citizenship Activity 4 blackline master on page 27. Invite a police officer to discuss with the class acquiring a driver's license and the importance of driver safety. **2.** Have students write and mail letters to the President that express opinions about the budget, defense, or security. Stress the importance of using facts to support their opinions. **3.** Have students write paragraphs that summarize the President's role in security, budget planning, and foreign policy.

Skill Builder: 1. Review the skills needed for reading a chart. Discuss the chart on page 190. After students complete the Skill Builder, have them choose any three nations and create charts using the same headings as the chart on page 190. **2.** Discuss and interpret the political cartoon on page 200. After students complete the Skill Builder, have them find a political cartoon in a newspaper or news magazine and share it with the class.

People in Government: Jimmy Carter spoke out strongly for human rights abroad and for civil rights in the United States while he was President. He imposed a grain embargo on the Soviet Union when that nation invaded Afghanistan. Have students write to the State Department for information about human rights abuses that the United States is opposing.

Focus on Government: Have students read Kennedy's inauguration speech aloud. If possible, play for them a recording of Kennedy giving that speech. Ask: What parts of that speech remain meaningful for today?

Chapter 17

Paying for Government

Objective: Students will learn: The United States has a free enterprise system where people must pay taxes to cover the government's expenses. The United States has a large debt.

New Vocabulary: profit, goods, services, consumers, income, regressive taxes, progressive taxes, debt

Vocabulary Activities: 1. Have students use the Graphic Organizer blackline master on page 30 to create a word web around the term *free enterprise*. **2.** Discuss with students the difference between progressive and regressive taxes, income and debt, and goods and services

Reading Words: benefit, capitalism, free enterprise, trillion, economy, medical care, defense, social security, disabilities, poultry, polluted, portion, expense, bond, billions, reduce

Review Words: agencies, executive, inspect, budget, debates, compromises, responsibilities, proposed

Pre-Reading Activities: 1. Have students name services that are paid for by the government. **2.** Brainstorm with students a list of reasons why people must pay taxes. **3.** Explain that United States Savings Bonds are a means of lending money to the government. Discuss why there is a difference between the purchase price of a bond and the price on maturity.

Post-Reading Activities: 1. Have students use the Graphic Organizer blackline master on page 30 to create a concept web around the term *taxes*. Have students use their concept webs to write paragraphs about taxes. **2.** Have students plan a real or hypothetical family budget for one week. Students should make one list that includes all income and another list that includes expenses. Encourage students to plan balanced budgets. **3.** Have the class write paragraphs that explain the main ideas of free enterprise.

Discussion Questions: 1. Discuss ways the government is involved with the economy in our free enterprise system. **2.** Why must all people who earn income pay personal income taxes? **3.** What kinds of taxes do you think are most fair? Why? **4.** Why is it difficult to plan the budget, and why are compromises needed for Congress to pass it? **5.** Why does the nation spend only 18% of the budget for programs such as education, parks, highways, and prisons? Why isn't more money available?

Chapter 18

Protecting the Nation

Objective: Students will learn: The American people are protected by the justice system and local police. The Department of Defense protects national security.

New Vocabulary: security, defense, prosecution, impartial, verdict, combat, intelligence

Vocabulary Activities: 1. Discuss the meaning of each word as it relates to the chapter. Explain that *security* refers to national security. *Defense* has two meanings in this chapter: the side during a trial that defends the accused; a term for the nation's military equipment and forces. **2.** Have students identify the root words of *security*, *defense*, *intelligence*, and *prosecution*.

Reading Words: commit, punishment, harsher, evidence, Federal Bureau of Investigation, Pentagon, civilian, Joint Chiefs of Staff, "first line of defense," register

Review Words: responsibilities, justice, criminals, guilty, guarantees, represent, jury, media, independent

Pre-Reading Activities: 1. Review with the class what has been learned in previous chapters about police, justice, and national defense. **2.** Have students make three lists of ways the government can provide protection for them. The lists should be titled *In the Community*, *In the Courts*, and *In the Nation*.

Post-Reading Activities: 1. Have students use the Graphic Organizer blackline master on page 31 to classify information about defense. Students should write *Protecting the Nation* in the large box and below that, the three headings: *local police*, *justice system*, *national defense*. Have students write related ideas in the spaces below each heading. Then have students use their organizers to write a three-paragraph summary about the three kinds of protection the nation needs. **2.** Divide the class into cooperative learning groups to follow current events for several days. Groups should create charts listing daily events that relate to the three kinds of protection needed by the nation. **3.** Have students write to the Department of Defense for information about how it protects national security. **4.** Invite a local judge or lawyer to discuss with the class the role of the courts in protecting an individual's legal rights.

Discussion Questions: 1. How can an accused person receive a fair trial? **2.** Why must a trial be held publicly and have an impartial jury in order to be fair? **3.** How do the F.B.I. and C.I.A. protect the nation? **4.** Why did the Framers want the military to be under civilian control? **5.** How do the Department of Defense and the National Security Council protect national security?

Chapter 19

Other Forms of Government

Objective: Students will learn: Parliamentary democracy is another form of democracy. It is practiced in Sweden. Sweden also has a socialist economy. Authoritarian governments, such as the absolute monarchy in Saudi Arabia and the Communist Party-controlled government of China, limit personal freedom.

New Vocabulary: monarchy, welfare, production contracts, surplus

Vocabulary Activities: 1. Have students identify the root words of *monarchy* and *production*. Have them derive meanings for *monarchy* and *production* using those root words. **2.** Have students use the vocabulary words in sentences.

Reading Words: Sweden, Saudi Arabia, China, Netherlands, Japan, Israel, Great Britain, Denmark, personal, ceremonies, minister, multiparty system, Socialist Party, socialism, economic system, features, allowance, pensions, retired

Review Words: separation of powers, Parliament, majority, executive, legislative, prime minister

Pre-Reading Activities: 1. Using a large world map, help students locate the eight nations mentioned in Chapter 19 and listed under Reading Words. **2.** Review the concept of free enterprise. Explain the meaning of communism and socialism to the class. **3.** Brainstorm with the class the differences between absolute and constitutional monarchies. **4.** Explain the meaning and importance of Islam.

Post-Reading Activities: 1. Have students use the Graphic Organizer blackline master on page 31 to categorize facts about Sweden, Saudi Arabia, and China. Have students write *Three Forms of Government* in the large box. Have students fill in the most important facts about each nation. Then have students use their organizers to write a summary about the three governments. **2.** Divide the class into cooperative learning groups to research the government of another nation. Have the groups present oral reports to the class. Have them organize the information they learn on a chart. **3.** Help students use the periodicals in the library to learn about the fall of communism in Eastern Europe during 1989 and 1990. How have governments changed since 1989?

Discussion Questions: 1. Discuss three ways that democracy in Sweden is different from that in the United States. **2.** How does Sweden's socialist economy differ from American free enterprise? In what ways are the systems alike? **3.** How does Islam affect Saudi Arabia? **4.** Why can China be called an authoritarian government? **5.** How does the Communist Party control China?

Chapter 20

In the Global Community

Objective: Students will learn: The United States develops and changes its foreign policy so it can work with other nations.

New Vocabulary: invasion, interdependence, conflict, human rights, isolationism, foreign aid, economic sanctions

Vocabulary Activities: 1. Have students identify the root words of *invasion*, *interdependence*, and *isolationism*. Have them define those words using the root meanings. **2.** Have students find the meaning of both parts of *foreign aid* and *economic sanctions* and then define those terms.

Reading Words: Iraq, Kuwait, Middle East, Eastern Europe, Soviet Union, Western Hemisphere, Hawaii, natural resources, freedom of the seas, economy, Monroe Doctrine, military base, superpower, Cold War, negotiate, ambassadors, appropriate, embassies, nuclear weapons, N.A.T.O., developing nations, agriculture, United Nations, Security Council, General Assembly

Review Words: policy, security, treaties, defense, declare war, environment

Pre-Reading Activities: 1. Have students locate on a world map all places mentioned in the chapter and listed under Reading Words. **2.** Brainstorm with the class about the meaning of foreign policy and its purpose. **3.** Have students work in pairs to find newspaper articles that show aspects of the current foreign policy of the United States. **4.** Discuss with the class the Persian Gulf War and the actions of the United States in that war.

Post-Reading Activities: 1. Have students use the Graphic Organizer blackline master on page 29 to compare and contrast present American foreign policy and early American foreign policy. **2.** Have each student find one newspaper article relating to United States foreign policy and present it to the class, explaining what it shows about U.S. foreign policy. **3.** Divide the class into cooperative learning groups to research one of the following topics: resources and goods the United States gets from other nations; the I.N.F. treaty; N.A.T.O.; O.A.S.; N.A.F.T.A.; the history of the Peace Corps; the beginning of the U.N. **4.** Create a flow chart with the class to show how American foreign policy has changed since 1787.

Discussion Questions: 1. What are the four goals of American foreign policy? **2.** How does the President plan foreign policy? **3.** Why do our foreign policies change? **4.** Discuss the six different methods that are used to carry out American foreign policy.

Note: A review activity covering Unit 5 is provided on page 42. A test covering Unit 5 is provided on page 43. The final book test is provided on pages 46, 47, and 48. An activity to help students review for the test is provided on pages 44 and 45.

Answer Key

Student Text

Chapter 1

Comprehension (Page 13)
1. Citizen of Athens
2. Citizen of Rome
3. British Prime Minister
4. King John

Vocabulary (Pages 13-14)
1. democracy
2. Population
3. citizen
4. jury
5. parliamentary government
6. Representatives
7. Parliament
8. prime minister

Critical Thinking (Page 14)
1. The Magna Carta
2. Direct Democracy
3. English Bill of Rights
4. Parliament
5. Representative Government

Chapter 2

Comprehension (Page 20)
Paragraphs will vary. Answers may include that because of abuses by King George and Parliament, Americans fought the American Revolution to gain independence.

Vocabulary (Pages 20-21)
1. laws
2. freedom
3. governor
4. represented
5. rules itself
6. approve

Critical Thinking (Page 21)
1. b
2. c
3. e
4. a
5. f
6. d

Chapter 3

Comprehension (Page 29)
1. d
2. a
3. c
4. b
5. e

Vocabulary (Page 29)
Paragraphs will vary. Answers may include that there is separation of powers into three branches: legislative, executive, and judicial; and that these branches check and balance one another.

Critical Thinking Analogies (Page 30)
1. Senate
2. judges
3. federal
4. Constitution
5. states

Critical Thinking--Fact or Opinion (Page 30)
1. F
2. FO. Students should write: the most important one is the right to property.
3. O
4. F
5. F

Skill Builder (Page 32)
1. 20, 45
2. The number of representatives went up.
3. The number from New York became fewer than the number from California.
4. It did not change for either state.
5. The population of New York has decreased while that of California has increased.

Chapter 4

Comprehension (Page 39)
1. What is the Preamble?
2. Why did the Framers divide the power among three branches?
3. What is the job of the President?
4. How can Congress override the President's veto?
5. What is the elastic clause?
6. Why would the President veto a bill?

Vocabulary (Pages 39-40)
1. Students should cross out: elastic. The three branches of government are the executive, the legislative, and the judicial branches.
2. Students should cross out: war. Three goals of the Constitution are justice, liberty, and peace.
3. Students should cross out: officials. The Preamble, articles, and amendments are all parts of the Constitution.
4. Students should cross out: appoint judges. Three powers of Congress are: declare war, make taxes, and approve treaties.

Critical Thinking (Page 40)
Student should check: 2, 5.

Skill Builder (Page 41)
1 – 6. Answers will vary.

Chapter 5

Vocabulary (Page 48)
1. guarantees
2. assembly
3. due process
4. double jeopardy
5. petition
6. naturalized
7. suffrage
8. terms

Comprehension (Pages 48-49)
1. Several states would not ratify the Constitution unless it had a Bill of Rights.
2. The First Amendment protects freedom of speech, freedom of religion, freedom of assembly, freedom of the press, and the freedom to petition the government.
3. People in a democracy need these freedoms in order to be part of government, an important aspect of democracy.
4. They guarantee due process, protection from double jeopardy, and the right to a fair and speedy trial.
5. The 13th, 14th, and 15th amendments helped African Americans.
6. They added the 26th Amendment so that 18-year-olds could vote.

Critical Thinking (Page 49)
Students should check: 4, 5, 7.

Chapter 6

Vocabulary (Page 60)
1. oath
2. census
3. bills
4. political party
5. adjourns
6. term
7. president *pro tempore*

Comprehension (Pages 60-61)
1. They must be at least 30 years old, have been citizens for 9 years, and live in the state they represent.
2. All districts must have about the same population, so when the populations in some districts grow, district lines must be redrawn.
3. A committee can approve it, change it, or let it die.
4. Sometimes a bill is important for the nation as a whole.
5. Members are elected by the people, and they often pass laws that the people want.
6. Answers will vary.

Critical Thinking (Page 61)
1. districts
2. senators
3. Speaker of the House
4. minority party
5. commerce

Chapter 7

Comprehension (Page 69)
Paragraphs will vary. Answers may include that the President has many jobs, such as commander in chief, chief diplomat, and chief executive. The President makes decisions about foreign policy, the budget, and new laws.

Vocabulary (Pages 69-70)
1. foreign nation
2. symbol

3. spending money   **4.** deal with other nations
5. committed a crime   **6.** bureaucracy

Critical Thinking (Page 70)
1. Commander in Chief   **2.** Chief Executive
3. Chief of State   **4.** Chief Diplomat
5. Chief Lawmaker

Skill Builder (Page 71)
1. Nixon had been accused of breaking the law.
2. They thought Nixon had abused his powers as chief executive and as party chief.
3. He thinks Nixon would have liked to have changed the Constitution.
4. He could have not included the part about impeachment.
5. Answers will vary.

Chapter 8 —————————————————
Comprehension (Page 82)
1. What are the Office of Management and Budget and the National Security Council?
2. What is the Department of Agriculture?
3. What is the Immigration and Naturalization Service?
4. What are civil service workers?

Vocabulary (Pages 82-83)
1. Students should cross out: Department of Defense. Three independent agencies are the Peace Corps, E.P.A., and C.I.A.
2. Students should cross out: Congress. The executive branch includes the Executive Office, the executive departments, and the independent agencies.
3. Students should cross out: foreign policy. Three jobs of the Department of the Treasury include stopping counterfeit money, collecting taxes, and protecting the President.
4. Students should cross out: food stamps. NASA spends money on research about computers and medicine and on spaceships such as Apollo 11.

Critical Thinking (Page 83)
1. F   **2.** O   **3.** O   **4.** FO Students should circle: the most important job in the executive branch.
5. F   **6.** FO Students should circle: whose work should be done by executive departments. **7.** F   **8.** O

Chapter 9 —————————————————
Comprehension (Page 90)
1. g   **2.** c   **3.** h   **4.** e
5. f   **6.** b   **7.** a   **8.** d

Critical Thinking (Pages 90-91)
Students should check: 1, 2, 5, 8.

Vocabulary (Page 91)
Paragraphs will vary. Answers may include that the court system must follow due process. It allows cases to be appealed. It overturns any laws that abuse the rights of the people.

Chapter 10 —————————————————
Comprehension (Page 99)
1. U.S. Representative   **2.** committee member
3. U.S. Senator   **4.** constituent   **5.** President

Vocabulary (Pages 99-100)
1. constituent   **2.** subcommittee   **3.** filibuster
4. debate   **5.** amend   **6.** conference committee

Critical Thinking (Page 100)
Students should check: 1, 5, 6, 7.

Skill Builder (Page 101)
1. Reagan, Carter, Ford, Nixon   **2.** Reagan
3. Reagan   **4.** Ford   **5.** Reagan
6. Reagan   **7.** Carter; He vetoed the fewest bills and had the fewest vetoes overridden.

Chapter 11 —————————————————
Vocabulary (Page 111)
Paragraphs will vary. Answers may include that state governments provide eduction, health care, and other services. They work to protect the environment.

Comprehension (Pages 111-112)
1. Each state is unique and so needs its own constitution to meet its needs.
2. State constitutions provide for limited government, checks and balances, and popular sovereignty. They all have a bill of rights and amendments.
3. They can establish local governments, create public school systems and court systems, pass laws, and collect taxes.
4. Answers will vary.
5. They must decide on the length of the school year and what subjects are studied, give money to special programs, and set graduation requirements.
6. Answers will vary.

Critical Thinking (Page 112)
1. c   **2.** e   **3.** a   **4.** f   **5.** d   **6.** b

Skill Builder (Page 113)
1. the South; the Northeast   **2.** 53,000   **3.** the South   **4.** the Northeast; When you add the total workers, it has the fewest.   **5.** the South; When you add the total workers it has the most.

Chapter 12 —————————————————
Vocabulary (Page 119)
1. apportioned   **2.** referendum   **3.** item veto
4. initiative   **5.** militia   **6.** sentence
7. criminal   **8.** due process

Comprehension (Pages 119-120)
1. How many houses do state legislatures have?
2. How is a bill passed in state government?
3. What is the initiative method?
4. When do states have referendums?
5. What are trial courts?

Critical Thinking (Page 120)
1. Governor   **2.** State Court System   **3.** Citizens Get Involved   **4.** Executive Powers of the Governor
5. Judicial Powers of the Governor

Chapter 13 —————————————————
Comprehension (Page 126)
Word order: Local, utilities, public transportation, county, officials, sheriff, district attorney, council-manager, manager

Vocabulary (Pages 126-127)
Paragraphs will vary. Answers may include that local governments provide utilities such as electricity, protection such as fire fighters, libraries, and public transportation.

Critical Thinking (Page 127)
1. FO Students should circle: and the city's government handled the emergency very well. **2.** FO Students should circle: but Queens' law promotes safer driving.
3. O **4.** F **5.** FO Students should circle: which is the correct way for states to be governed. **6.** O
7. F **8.** O **9.** F **10.** F

Skill Builder (Page 128)
1. 8% **2.** public utilities **3.** police and fire protection **4.** parks and recreation **5.** police and fire protection **6.** parks and recreation
7. Workers in Police and Fire Protection receive a larger percentage of the payments compared to the percent of workers they represent, while workers in Parks and Recreation receive a smaller percentage of the payments.

Chapter 14 ───────────────────
Comprehension (Page 140)
1. candidate **2.** nonvoter **3.** average voter
4. third-party leader **5.** party volunteer

Vocabulary (Pages 140-141)
1. candidate **2.** platform **3.** polling place
4. registration **5.** third party **6.** transportation
7. average

Critical Thinking (Page 141)
Students should check: 1, 2, 3, 7.

Skill Builder (Page 142)
1. 18–19 years old **2.** 35–44 and 45–64 years old
3. 61% **4.** 4% **5.** Only half of the registered voters who were 20–24 years old actually voted in the 1992 election.

Chapter 15 ───────────────────
Vocabulary (Page 150)
Paragraphs will vary. Answers may include that candidates hold fund-raising events and use public funds in order to pay for their campaigns. Through public opinion polls, they are able to tell what the public opinion is and then use propaganda and the media to influence public opinion.

Comprehension (Pages 150-151)
1. What are primary elections?
2. What happens at a national convention?
3. Why do candidates have to raise so much money?
4. What is used to influence public opinion?
5. What is propaganda?
6. Why do campaign managers take public opinion polls?
7. What happens on election day?

Critical Thinking (Page 151)
Students should check: 2, 3, 7, 8.

Chapter 16 ───────────────────
Comprehension (Page 159)
1. Business interest groups work on behalf of the workers they represent. Issues interest groups work for one specific issue and for the people who believe in that issue. Public interest groups work for the good of all people.
2. People can work for interest groups to help pass laws that concern them.
3. Answers will vary.
4. Answers will vary.

5. PACs give money to candidates and run campaigns for candidates.
6. Answers will vary.

Vocabulary (Pages 159-160)
1. Students should cross out: senators. Interest groups, PACs, and lobbyists all work to influence lawmakers.
2. Students should cross out: Democratic Party. Friends of the Earth, the League of Women Voters, and the National Education Association are all interest groups.
3. Students should cross out: voter registration. Newspaper ads, television commericals, and letter writing are all ways that lobbyists influence public opinion.
4. Students should cross out: discriminate. People pressure, lobby, and influence lawmakers to pass laws for their interest groups.

Critical Thinking (Page 160)
1. public interest group **2.** PACs **3.** influence
4. N.O.W. **5.** wildlife

Skill Builder (Page 161)
1. the Democrats; 1981-82 **2.** 1985-86
3. 1985-86 **4.** 2 million more
5. Contributions went up.
6. They have gone up and down.

Chapter 17 ───────────────────
Comprehension (Page 173)
Paragraphs will vary. Answers may include that people pay taxes to cover government programs such as highways and education. Agencies need money to carry out laws. The government uses money to pay for its debt.

Vocabulary (Pages 173-174)
1. profits **2.** businesses **3.** make
4. spends **5.** businesses **6.** sales tax
7. high incomes **8.** borrowed

Critical Thinking (Page 174)
1. c **2.** e **3.** f **4.** d **5.** a **6.** b

Chapter 18 ───────────────────
Comprehension (Page 180)
1. e **2.** h **3.** f **4.** c
5. d **6.** a **7.** b **8.** g

Vocabulary (Pages 180-181)
Paragraphs will vary. Answers may include that the government protects people's rights when they have been accused of a crime. It protects the nation by collecting intelligence about other nations and by providing for a strong military through the armed forces.

Critical Thinking (Page 181)
1. Fair Trial **2.** F.B.I. **3.** National Security Council **4.** Military **5.** Air Force **6.** C.I.A.

Chapter 19 ───────────────────
Comprehension (Page 188)
Word order: parliamentary, socialist, welfare, communist, revolution, government, Communist Party, personal, speech, royal

Vocabulary (Pages 188-189)
1. Students should cross out: free enterprise. An authoritarian government, constitutional monarchy, and

a parliamentary democracy are all types of government.

2. Students should cross out: freedom of religion. In Saudi Arabia, there is no constitution, and it is an absolute monarchy ruled by the royal family.
3. Students should cross out: China. The United States, Great Britain, and Sweden are all democracies.
4. Students should cross out: freedom of speech. China has an authoritarian government and a communist economy in which workers must fulfill production contracts.
5. Students should cross out: low taxes. The welfare system in Sweden provides for paid vacations, allowances for children, and free health care.

Critical Thinking (Page 189)
1. F 2. O 3. FO Students should circle: but it is worth paying high taxes to get the benefits. 4. F
5. F 6. O 7. O 8. F 9. FO Students should circle: and the government should have listened to the demands of the students.

Skill Builder (Page 190)
1. China has the largest and Sweden has the smallest.
2. Communist, free enterprise, socialist
3. China
4. Answers will vary. 5. Answers will vary.

Chapter 20
Comprehension (Page 198)
1. George Washington 2. President Monroe
3. Secretary of State 4. member of Congress
5. Peace Corps volunteer 6. soldier

Vocabulary (Pages 198-199)
1. invasion 2. human rights 3. conflicts
4. superpower 5. interdependence 6. foreign aid
7. alliance 8. economic sanctions

Critical Thinking (Page 199)
Students should check: 1, 4, 5, 7.

Skill Builder (Page 200)
1. The two men are fighting.
2. It stands for Iraq's invasion of Kuwait.
3. The United Nations is talking.
4. They refer to Iraq's invasion of Kuwait.
5. They depend on George Bush to protect them from Iraq.
6. The Arabs would make more money on oil if the prices went up.
7. The cartoonist thinks that the U.N. didn't have much power in the Persian Gulf crisis.

Blackline Masters Answer Key

Unit 1 Review (Pages 32-33)
Across: 1. civil rights **5.** veto **6.** checks
7. popular **10.** Preamble **13.** guarantees
15. compromises
Down: 1. Constitution **2.** represent **3.** senators
4. declare **8.** abuse **9.** amendments
11. democracy **12.** assembly **14.** ratify

Unit 1 Test (Page 34)
1. b 2. b 3. b 4. c 5. b
6. c 7. b 8. c 9. b 10. b

Unit 2 Review (Pages 35-36)
Across: 2. adjourns **5.** opposes **6.** majority
8. budget **9.** committee **11.** precedents
13. taxes **15.** agencies **16.** judicial
Down: 1. commander **3.** justice **4.** speaker
7. executive **10.** segregation **12.** session
14. security

Unit 2 Test (Page 37)
1. b 2. a 3. b 4. b 5. a
6. b 7. a 8. c 9. b 10. a

Unit 3 Review (Page 38)
1. Answers may include: establish local government; create a public school system; create a state court system; pass laws; collect taxes.
2. Amendments have been added to state constitutions because states must change to meet the needs of their people.
3. Answers may include: prepare state budgets; make state policies; call up the militia; appoint officials; propose bills and approve or veto laws; appoint state judges; pardon convicted people.
4. A governor might use the item veto to allow part of a bill to become law while vetoing another part.
5. The initiative method allows citizens to propose laws. The referendum method allows citizens to vote on certain kinds of laws.
6. In some states, judges are appointed to state courts by the government; in most states, judges are elected.
7. Trials courts hear civil and criminal cases. Courts of appeal decide whether a trial court followed due process. The state supreme court is the highest court in the state.
8. Local governments meet the needs of the people by providing services and solving local problems.
9. County governments carry out state laws; pass laws that meet local needs; collect taxes to pay for services such as police protection, libraries, etc.
10. A mayor-council city government is elected; the mayor is the chief executive, and the council is the legislature. A council-manager city government has an elected city council, which chooses the manager to plan the budget, control money, and carry out policies set by the council.

Unit 3 Test (Page 39)
1. c 2. b 3. c 4. b 5. a
6. c 7. b 8. a 9. a 10. b

Unit 4 Review (Page 40)
1. Jobs of political parties include: set goals for the nation by developing party platforms; be involved in elections; inform the public about candidates and their party platforms; identify problems they think the government should solve; put party platform ideas into action through elected members; check that other parties follow through on promises.
2. Third parties form because they have a different idea of how government should be organized, they support one important issue, or they don't agree with either of the majority parties.
3. A voter must be 18, a citizen, a resident of the state in which he or she is voting, and (except in North Dakota) registered.

4. Answers may include: they lack knowledge about candidates and issues; they feel their vote doesn't count; they don't care who wins or loses; they want to but can't because of disability, hardship, or lack of transportation; they dislike all candidates or feel they are all equal; they don't feel a strong tie to a political party; they are not registered.

5. At primary elections, voters choose delegates to the convention to vote on a candidate. At national conventions, delegates nominate one person to be the party's candidate, and they decide on the party's platform.

6. The media runs ads, shows debates; shows activities of candidates, and announces results of polls.

7. Public funds make it easier for candidates to pay for campaigns and to become candidates in primaries.

8. Business interest groups work to make sure their businesses grow and make money. (A.M.A.) Issue interest groups try to influence government to support issues that concern the members. (M.A.D.D.) Public interest groups work for the interest of all people. (League of Women Voters)

9. Lobbyists influence government by bringing information to members of Congress, by using the media to inform the public, and by providing information to members of the interest groups.

10. Congress has passed laws to limit the power of interest groups so they will not gain too much control over government decisions and actions.

Unit 4 Test (Page 41)

| 1. c | 2. b | 3. a | 4. b | 5. c |
| 6. a | 7. c | 8. c | 9. c | 10. c |

Unit 5 Review (Page 42)

1. Answers will vary.

2. Executive departments and agencies send their budget needs to the Office of Management and Budget. The President and the O.M.B. plan the budget based on those needs. Congress approves the budget, usually after changes and compromises.

3. The personal income tax provides the most money.

4. The government provides more than it has money to pay for so it has borrowed billions of dollars.

5. Answers will vary.

6. The Army fights on land; the Navy fights on sea, with one branch, the Marines, who fight on land; and the Air Force fights in the air.

7. An absolute monarchy has a king or queen with almost complete power. In a constitutional monarchy, the king or queen has only the powers allowed by the constitution.

8. Answers will vary.

9. Goals might include: protecting the security of Americans and American businesses in all parts of the world; protecting the interests of the nation; improving the economy through international trade; promoting democracy, independence, and human rights; promoting world peace.

10. Answers will vary.

Unit 5 Test (Page 43)

| 1. c | 2. a | 3. b | 4. a | 5. a |
| 6. c | 7. b | 8. a | 9. a | 10. a |

Final Review (Pages 44-45)

1. Representative government is a government in which the people elect leaders to represent them in making laws for the nation.

2. King George imposed unfair taxes on the colonies, and he did not allow the colonists to help write their own laws.

3. Answers will vary.

4. It had to protect people's natural rights; limit the powers of government; provide for popular sovereignty; separate the powers; provide for checks and balances; and divide government between federal and state governments.

5. Answers will vary.

6. A census is taken to count the population. The number of representatives from each state may change.

7. Answers will vary.

8. Judicial review is the power of the Supreme Court to find government actions or laws unconstitutional.

9. Congress can override the veto with a two-thirds vote in both houses, or it can prepare a compromise bill that the President would sign.

10. States have rewritten their constitutions to meet the changing needs of their people.

11. Local governments are created to provide services for communities, carry out state laws, and make laws for local protection and services.

12. The steps are: announcing as candidate; primary election; campaign; national convention; election day.

13. Candidates spend money on advertising, travel, offices, and campaign workers' salaries.

14. Answers will vary.

15. Executive departments and agencies send their budget needs to the Office of Management and Budget. The President and the O.M.B. plan the budget based on those needs. Congress approves the budget, usually after changes and compromises.

16. The rights of an accused person are protected through his or her right to a lawyer, to knowledge about charges and evidence, and to a fair and public trial by an impartial jury. The prosecution and defense must follow the same court rules.

17. National security is protected through the Department of Defense, C.I.A., treaties, and alliances.

18. An absolute monarchy has a king or queen with almost complete power. In a constitutional monarchy, the king or queen has only the powers allowed by the constitution.

19. All nations depend on one another for trade and for peace.

20. Answers should include three of the following: treaties, the Peace Corps, the United Nations, negotiations, alliances, military force.

Final Test (Pages 46-48)

1. a	2. a	3. b	4. a	5. b
6. a	7. c	8. b	9. b	10. c
11. b	12. c	13. a	14. c	15. c
16. c	17. b	18. a	19. a	20. c
21. a	22. b	23. a	24. b	25. a
26. b	27. a	28. c	29. a	30. c
31. c	32. b	33. a	34. c	

Government Addresses

The President of the United States
1600 Pennsylvania Ave. NW
Washington, D.C. 20500

United States Senator
United States Senate
Washington, D.C. 20510

United States Representative
United States House of Representatives
Washington, D.C. 20515

Attorney General
Constitution Ave. & 10th St. NW
Washington, D.C. 20530

Secretary of Defense
The Pentagon
Washington, D.C. 20301

Secretary of Education
400 Maryland Ave. SW
Washington, D.C. 20202

Secretary of the Interior
1849 C St. between 18th & 19th Sts. NW
Washington, D.C. 20240

Secretary of Labor
200 Constitution Ave. NW
Washington, D.C. 20210

Secretary of State
2201 C St. NW
Washington, D.C. 20520

Secretary of Transportation
400 7th St. SW
Washington, D.C. 20590

Secretary of the Treasury
1500 Pennsylvania Ave. NW
Washington, D.C. 20220

Consumer Product Safety Commission
Washington, D.C. 20207

Environmental Protection Agency
Public Affairs
401 M Street, SW
Washington, D.C. 20460

Federal Election Commission
999 E St. NW
Washington, D.C. 20463

General Accounting Office
441 G St. NW
Washington, D.C. 20548

Government Printing Office
North Capitol and H Sts. NW
Washington, D.C. 20401

NASA
300 E Street SW
2 Independence Square
Washington, D.C. 20546

Peace Corps
Volunteer Program Information
1990 K Street NW
Washington, D.C. 20526

Postal Service
Consumer Affairs
475 L'Enfant Plaza, SW
Washington, D.C. 20260

Small Business Administration
409 3rd Street SW
Washington, D.C. 20416

United States Information Agency
301 4th St. SW
Washington, D.C. 20547

Name _____

Citizenship Activity 1 ▰▰▰▰▰▰▰▰
Learning About Your Members of Congress

We depend on our senators and representatives to represent us in Congress. By learning about their voting records and committee work, we can tell what kind of job they are doing. To obtain information about members of Congress, we can use the following reference books:

1. *The Congressional Directory* has a brief biography about each member, including committee membership, party membership, and professional and political experience.

2. *The Congressional Quarterly Almanac* provides information on the voting record, seniority in Congress, professional experience, and religion of each senator and representative.

3. The *Almanac of American Politics* lists members of Congress according to their states. Information includes photographs, voting records on key bills, sources of campaign money, support by interest groups, and family background.

4. *The World Almanac of United States Politics* includes biographical information on each member, such as religion, family background, committees, and voting records.

There are other ways to obtain information about members of Congress. You can request their official biographies from their offices in your state. Read news articles about congressional activities to learn what your members of Congress are doing. Interest groups also provide information about senators and representatives.

On Your Own ━━━━━━━━━━━━━━━━━━━━━━━━━━━━━━━━━

1. Write a letter to one of your senators or representatives to request a copy of their official biography.

2. On a separate piece of paper, create a profile of one of your members of Congress. Use one or more reference books and include the following information: date of birth, marital status, number of children, occupation, political party, date elected, committee membership, voting record on three recent bills, and authorship of bills.

Name _____

Citizenship Activity 2
Understanding Propaganda

Propaganda is used to influence public opinion. It is used in advertising to persuade people to buy different kinds of products. In politics, propaganda is used to persuade citizens to vote for certain candidates.

A responsible citizen must be able to separate propaganda from the correct facts about political candidates. To recognize propaganda, we must understand the different methods that are used to influence public opinion.

Three Propaganda Methods

1. **Testimonials** are statements made by well-known people that encourage citizens to vote for a candidate. For example, in 1988, President Reagan said George Bush was the best candidate. Many people listened to Reagan and voted for Bush. Many advertisers use famous people in their ads. What companies have Michael Jordan in their ads?

2. The **plain folks** method tells people that the candidate is just like other ordinary Americans. President Jimmy Carter used this method during his campaign when he wore jeans and played softball when the media was present. This method makes people feel the candidate will understand their problems. Advertisers use this method often because most buyers are "plain folks."

3. **Name calling** is a method used to make an opponent less popular. The opponent is given unpopular labels such as racist, dishonest, or uncaring. This method gives the opponent a very poor image. Advertisers tell you that other similar products are expensive or unhealthy. In this way, they hope you will buy their product.

On Your Own

1. Find product advertisements in a newspaper or magazine that are examples of each type of propaganda method. On a separate sheet of paper, explain how each ad uses the propaganda method to influence consumers.

2. Find one example of each propaganda method used in television commercials. On a separate piece of paper, briefly describe the ad and explain why you think that method was used.

Citizenship Activity 3
Understanding the Voting Process

The Constitution allows each state to write its own voting laws, but the voting process is similar in every state. Let's look at different steps in the voting process.

1. **Voter Registration**   People register to vote by completing a voter registration form. These forms can be found at public libraries and at board of election offices in the state. Registration can be done in person at an election office or by mailing a completed registration form to a state election office. The information on the registration form must include date of birth, address, length of time living at the address, and citizenship information. Remember also to sign the form!

2. **At the Polling Place**   A person can vote in only one assigned polling place. Every voter must sign in before voting. Officers check each person's name in a book that contains the voter registration information of everyone assigned to that polling place. Then, each person signs his or her name in the voting book. An official checks that the signature matches the one on the registration form. In this way, officers are sure that each person votes only once. Often, officers from both parties are there to make sure the voting is fair.

3. **Voting**   After signing in, voters take a ballot into a voting booth. Voters can take as much time to vote as they need. When they have voted, voters put their ballot in a locked ballot box. Voting is done in secret. No one can know how you vote unless you tell them.

4. **Differences in Procedures**   Three different methods are used for voting. In most places, people vote by using an electric voting machine or a punch card. Many places still use ballot cards that are marked with a pencil.

On Your Own

Call or write to the League of Women Voters. Find out the procedures in your state for registering and voting. Get a voter registration form from your local library. Read it to see what information is required.

Citizenship Activity 4 ▰▰▰▰▰▰▰▰▰▰▰▰▰▰▰▰▰▰▰▰
Dealing With the Government

As people become adults, they have more occasions to interact with the government. Let's look at three ways Americans deal with their government.

1. **Getting Social Security**   Taxes on money you earn go to social security. That money is given to people who retire, are disabled, or who depend on someone who has died. Someday you will get money from social security. Every person who has a job or a bank account must have a social security number. The law now requires every child who is past the age of one to have a social security number. If you do not yet have a number, you should apply for one. You can get an application from your nearest social security office. For more information, write to: Social Security Administration, 6401 Security Boulevard, Baltimore, Maryland 21235.

2. **Registering for the Draft**   The draft is when men are forced to serve in the military for a certain length of time. Today all members of the American military are volunteers, but the government keeps a list of men who could be drafted if it becomes necessary. All men who were born after 1960 must register with the Selective Service System. To register, men complete a form at their post office within 30 days after they turn 18. It is a crime for men not to register. For more information, write to: Selective Service System, National Headquarters, 1023 31st Street N.W., Washington, D.C. 20435.

3. **Obtaining a Driver's License**   Each state has its own tests for granting licenses. In every state, a new driver must pass a written test and a road test. To find out how to get a driver's license, call or write the Department of Motor Vehicles in your state. You can also ask for information about car registration and safety inspections.

On Your Own ▬▬▬▬▬▬▬▬▬▬▬▬▬▬▬▬▬▬▬▬▬▬▬▬▬▬

1. Write to the Department of Motor Vehicles to find out your state's requirements for both car registration and obtaining a driver's license.
2. Write a letter to the Social Security Administration for information on the types of benefits it offers.

Citizenship Activity 5 ▆▆▆▆▆▆▆▆▆▆▆▆▆▆▆
Using the Newspaper

Reading the newspaper is the best way to learn about government activities and decisions that take place each day. There are seven places in a newspaper to find information about government.

1. The **Front Page** describes important events and government actions of the day. Often these news stories are finished on later pages of the paper.

2. The **International News** section describes events around the world. It includes news about American foreign policy.

3. The **National News** section describes events in the nation. These stories often describe actions of the federal government.

4. The **Local News** section includes articles about the state and local governments.

5. The **Business News** section describes news about banking, foreign trade, and business events. It includes information about government policies on business.

6. The **Editorial** section has editorials that express the opinions of the newspaper's editors. These editorials often support or criticize recent government decisions, suggest new government policies, or recommend new types of laws for all levels of government. There are also editorials by writers in other parts of the country. In this way, different opinions about an issue are printed.

7. The **Letters to the Editor** section has letters from readers who agree or disagree with the opinions expressed in recent editorials. Often these letters are about news stories that appear in the paper. Reading these letters is one way of finding out what other people are thinking.

On Your Own ▬▬▬▬▬▬▬▬▬▬▬▬▬▬▬▬▬▬▬▬▬▬▬▬▬▬▬

1. Find one article, editorial, or letter that contains information about government. Be prepared to explain the article, editorial, or letter to the class.

2. Write a letter to the editor of a local newspaper. Tell why you agree or disagree with a recent editorial. Give at least three reasons for your point of view.

Graphic Organizer 1: Venn Diagram

Use this Venn diagram to compare and contrast information. Write above each circle the topics you are comparing. Write on the right and left the facts that are only about each topic. In the middle, write the facts that are common to both topics.

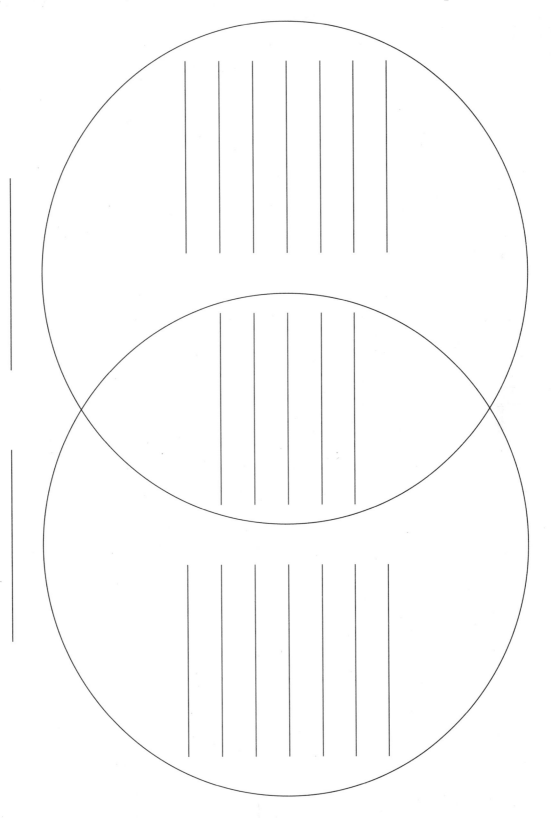

Graphic Organizer 2: Concept Web

A concept web is used to make connections between ideas. It can be used in four ways. It can show how vocabulary words are linked to a main idea. It can show the conclusions that can be drawn from a main idea. It can show how facts support a main idea. And it can show the effects of an action.

Write the main idea or the action in the middle. Then write the vocabulary, conclusions, supporting facts, or effects on the surrounding lines.

Name _____

Graphic Organizer 3: Organizing Map ███████████████

An organizing map is used to organize information or to put information into categories. It can be used in two ways. **(1)** Write the title in the small box at the top. **(2)** Write the main idea in the large box. Then write in the boxes below the information that is connected in different ways to the main idea. **(3)** Divide the large box into three parts. Write the title of a category in each part. Then write in the boxes below facts or ideas that belong to each category.

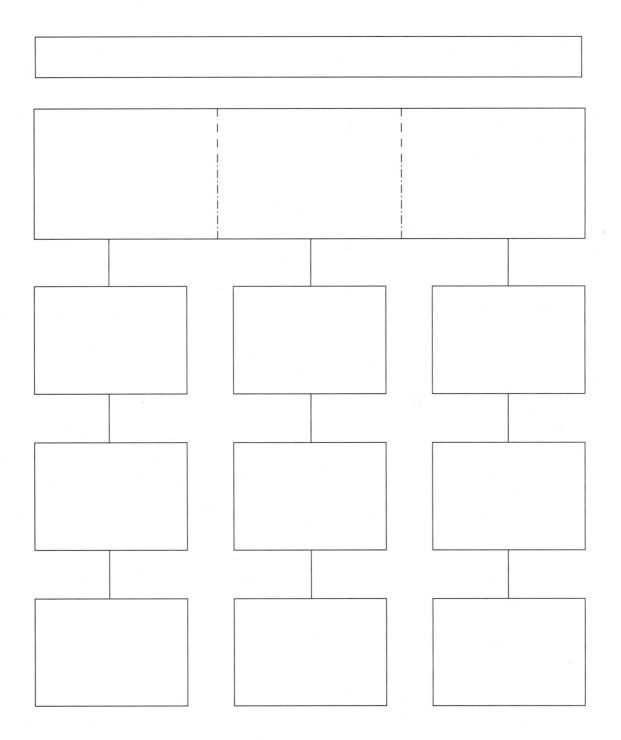

Unit 1 Review

Each sentence below has a missing word. Choose the missing word for each sentence from the words in the boxes. Then write each word in the right place on the puzzle.

ACROSS

1. Martin Luther King, Jr., worked to win _____ for all Americans.

5. The President can _____ a bill passed by Congress in order to keep it from becoming law.

6. Each branch of government limits the power of the other branches through _____ and balances.

7. The United States has _____ sovereignty because the government gets its power from the people.

10. The goals of the government are explained in the _____ of the Constitution.

13. The Bill of Rights _____ many rights to every American.

15. The Framers had to make many _____ before the Constitution was finished.

DOWN

1. The _____ is the supreme law of the land.

2. In American democracy, people vote for leaders to _____ them in the government.

3. Members of Congress are _____ and representatives.

4. Only Congress has the power to _____ war.

8. The Framers wanted the Constitution to prevent the _____ of power by the government.

9. Twenty-seven _____ have been added to the Constitution since 1787.

11. The world's first _____ began in Athens, Greece, more than 2,000 years ago.

12. The First Amendment protects the right of _____ , so people are free to gather and speak out against the government.

14. Once the Framers had written the Constitution, nine of the thirteen states had to _____ it.

Name _____

ACROSS

Preamble   civil rights   checks   popular
guarantees   compromises   veto

DOWN

declare   Constitution   democracy   abuse   senators
represent   assembly   ratify   amendments

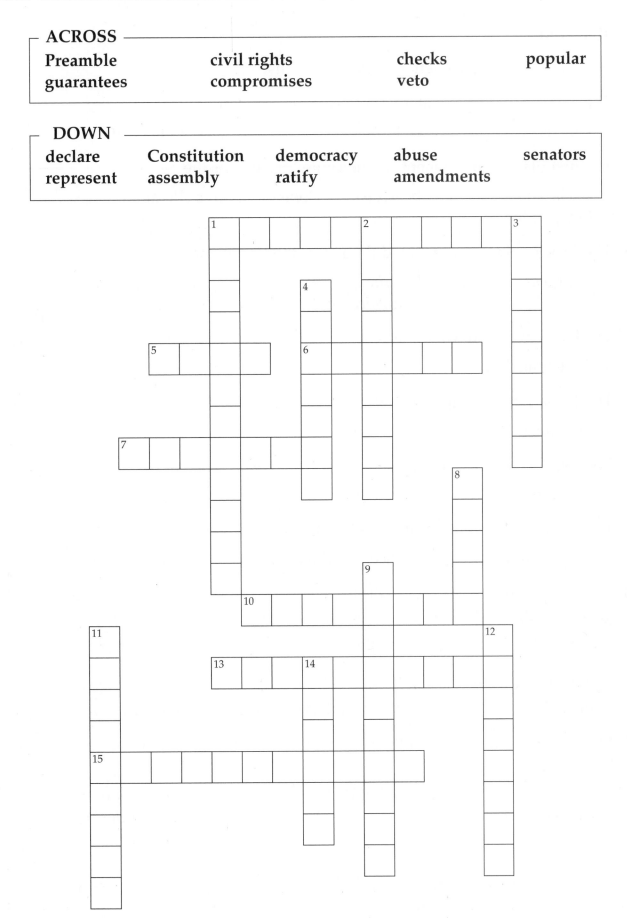

Unit 1 Test

Draw a circle around the letter of the correct answer.

1. The world's first representative government began in _____ .

   a. Athens   b. Rome   c. Great Britain

2. The first plan of government for the United States was the _____ .

   a. Declaration of   b. Articles of Confederation c. Preamble
   Independence

3. The Articles of Confederation did not give the United States a _____ .

   a. Congress   b. strong central   c. state government
                        government

4. The Framers did not want the government to have _____ .

   a. three branches   b. popular sovereignty   c. a king and queen

5. The Three-Fifths Compromise was about _____ .

   a. senators   b. slavery   c. courts

6. The Framers planned the _____ branch to interpret the laws.

   a. legislative   b. executive   c. judicial

7. The power of each branch of government is limited by _____ .

   a. due process   b. checks and balances   c. popular sovereignty

8. The first paragraph of the Constitution, which states the goals of American government, is called _____ .

   a. Article 1   b. the Bill of Rights   c. the Preamble

9. Women received the right to vote in the _____ .

   a. Preamble   b. Nineteenth Amendment c. Bill of Rights

10. Many personal freedoms and the rights of accused people are protected by the _____ .

    a. Articles of   b. Bill of Rights   c. Declaration of
    Confederation   Independence

Unit 2 Review

Each sentence below has a missing word. Choose the missing word for each sentence from the words in the boxes. Then write each word in the right place on the puzzle.

ACROSS

2. A session of Congress _____ when both houses agree that they have finished their work.

5. If a President _____ a bill, he can veto it.

6. The Senate and the House of Representatives must have a _____ of votes in order to pass a bill.

8. The President and the Office of Management and Budget plan an annual _____ for how the government will spend money.

9. A bill is often sent to a _____ , where it will be studied and perhaps returned to the House or Senate for approval.

11. Supreme Court decisions create guidelines, or _____ , for judging future cases.

13. The Department of the Treasury coins money and collects federal _____ .

15. The executive department has many _____ that carry out the laws of Congress.

16. The Supreme Court has the right of _____ review, so it decides whether laws are constitutional.

DOWN

1. As the _____ in chief, the President leads the branches of the military.

3. The judicial branch works to see that all people receive _____ .

4. The leader of the House of Representatives is the _____ of the House.

7. The President is the leader of the _____ branch.

10. The *Brown v. Topeka Board of Education* Supreme Court decision ended _____ in schools.

12. The President can call a special _____ of Congress to deal with business that cannot wait until the regular session begins.

14. The President and the National Security Council work together to protect national _____ .

Name _____

ACROSS
| committee | taxes | majority | opposes | adjourns |
| judicial | agencies | budget | precedents | |

DOWN
| justice | executive | commander | segregation |
| session | security | Speaker | |

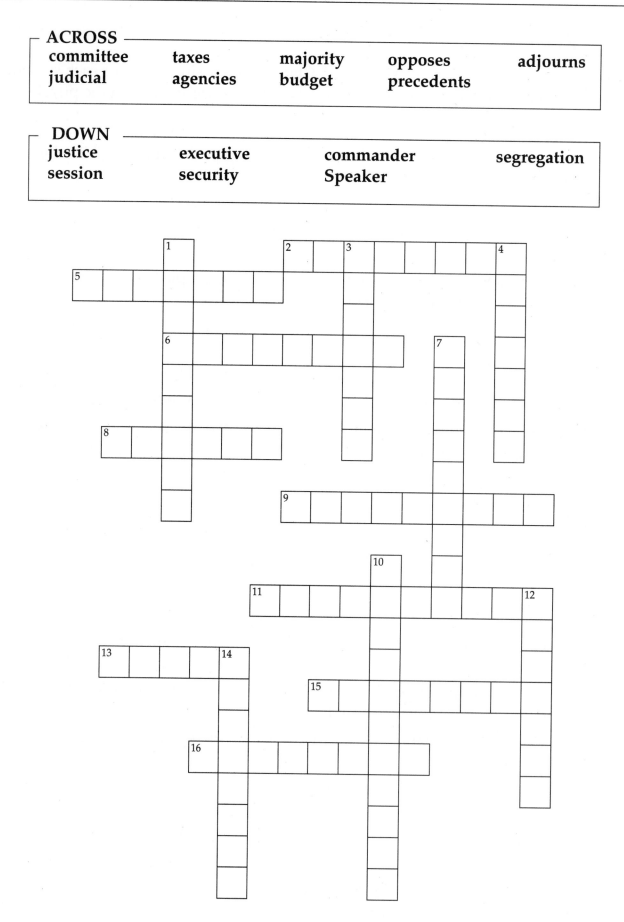

Copyright © 1997 Steck-Vaughn Company. *American Government: Freedom, Rights, Responsibilities*

Name _____

Unit 2 Test

Draw a circle around the letter of the correct answer.

1. The main job of Congress is to _____ .

   a. collect taxes   b. make laws   c. add amendments

2. The number of representatives from a state depends on that state's _____ .

   a. population   b. lawmakers   c. judicial branch

3. When all business is completed, Congress _____ .

   a. votes   b. adjourns   c. takes an oath

4. The _____ serves as president of the Senate.

   a. President   b. Vice President   c. Chief Justice

5. Only the _____ branch can declare war.

   a. legislative   b. executive   c. judicial

6. As Chief of State, the President must _____ .

   a. appoint ambassadors   b. attend ceremonies   c. veto bills

7. The White House _____ helps the President carry out daily business.

   a. staff   b. bureau   c. department

8. Decisions made by the _____ cannot be appealed or overturned.

   a. District Court   b. Court of Appeals   c. Supreme Court

9. The *Brown v. Topeka Board of Education* Supreme Court decision forced states to pass _____ laws.

   a. segregation   b. desegregation   c. environmental protection

10. House and Senate committees _____ most proposed bills.

   a. kill   b. rewrite   c. pass

Name _____

Unit 3 Review

Write one or more sentences to answer each question.

1. What are five powers of state governments? _____

_____

2. Why have many amendments been added to state constitutions? _____

_____

3. What are two jobs of a governor? _____

_____

4. Why would a governor use the item veto? _____

_____

5. What are the initiative and referendum methods? _____

_____

_____

6. How are judges appointed to state courts? _____

_____

7. Describe three kinds of state courts. _____

_____

8. What is the job of local government? _____

_____

_____

9. What do county governments do for communities? _____

_____

10. What are the differences between a mayor-council city government and a

council-manager city government? _____

_____

_____

Name _____

Unit 3 Test

Draw a circle around the letter of the correct answer.

1. State governments do not have the power to _____ .

   a. establish courts   b. create public school   c. print money
                               systems

2. The largest agency in every state government is the _____ agency.

   a. police   b. education   c. justice

3. State governments have the power to _____ .

   a. declare war   b. manufacture coins   c. make taxes

4. Every state is apportioned into districts to give all people _____ .

   a. lower taxes   b. equal representation   c. more representation

5. Many states allow citizens to help make laws through _____ .

   a. initiatives   b. courts and hearings   c. protests and marches
      and referendums

6. A governor has the power to _____ .

   a. hear court cases   b. make foreign treaties   c. pardon crimes

7. Every state but Nebraska has a legislature with _____ houses.

   a. one   b. two   c. three

8. The lowest state courts are _____ .

   a. trial courts   b. intermediate courts   c. state supreme courts
                               of appeal

9. Garbage collection and safe drinking water are services provided by the _____ government.

   a. local   b. state   c. federal

10. The guidelines for a city government are called the city _____ .

   a. constitution   b. charter   c. amendments

Name _____

Unit 4 Review

Write one or more sentences to answer each question.

1. What are four jobs that political parties do? _____

_____

2. What are two reasons that third parties form? _____

_____

3. What are the four requirements a person must meet in order to vote? _____

_____

_____

4. What are three reasons that many people decide not to vote? _____

_____

5. What are the purposes of primary elections and national political conventions?

_____

_____

6. How does the media try to influence public opinion during a campaign? _____

_____

_____

7. How do public funds help political candidates? _____

_____

8. What are three types of interest groups? Give an example of each. _____

_____

_____

9. How do lobbyists work to influence government? _____

_____

10. Why has Congress passed laws to limit the power of interest groups? _____

_____

Name _____

Unit 4 Test

Draw a circle around the letter of the correct answer.

1. One requirement for voting in every state is that a person be a _____ .

   a. college graduate   b. lawyer   c. citizen

2. In all states except North Dakota, one requirement for voting is _____ .

   a. paying a tax   b. registration   c. education

3. At the national convention, each political party can _____ one candidate to be on the ballot in the general election.

   a. nominate   b. hire   c. call

4. In order to win a political party's nomination, a candidate must win the most _____ .

   a. votes from all parties b. delegate votes   c. votes from Congress

5. All candidates can use _____ to pay for their campaigns.

   a. budgets   b. tax money   c. public funds

6. Candidates depend on _____ to find out whether their campaign methods are winning votes.

   a. public opinion polls b. political parties   c. PACs

7. Political campaigns are expensive because they often last _____ .

   a. a few weeks   b. a few months   c. a year or more

8. Interest groups hire professionals called _____ to influence government leaders.

   a. attorneys   b. campaign managers   c. lobbyists

9. It is against the law for interest groups to _____ lawmakers to pass laws.

   a. pressure   b. influence   c. force

10. During an election campaign, a PAC cannot _____ .

   a. contribute money to   b. run its own campaign   c. contribute more than
      many candidates   for a candidate $5,000 to a campaign

Unit 5 Review

Write one or more sentences to answer each question.

1. What are two ways that government is involved in the economy? _____

   _____

2. How is the budget made? _____

   _____

3. What kind of tax provides the most money for the federal government? _____

   _____

4. Why is it difficult for the United States to have a balanced budget? _____

   _____

5. Explain three things that must be done in order for a person to have a fair trial. ____

   _____

   _____

6. Describe the three branches of the military. _____

   _____

7. What is the difference between an absolute monarchy and a constitutional

   monarchy? _____

   _____

8. What are two ways that the governments of Saudi Arabia and China limit the

   freedom of their people? _____

   _____

9. Explain four foreign-policy goals of the United States. _____

   _____

10. Describe three ways that American foreign policy is carried out. _____

   _____

   _____

Name _____

Unit 5 Test

Draw a circle around the letter of the correct answer.

1. In a free enterprise economy, decisions about how to earn money and use profits are made by the _____ .

   a. state governments   b. federal government   c. people

2. The largest amount of tax money in the United States budget comes from the _____ .

   a. personal income tax   b. corporate income tax   c. social security tax

3. The largest expense in the United States budget is _____ .

   a. transportation   b. social security, Medicare,   c. interest on the national
      and ecucation   and other benefits   debt

4. A fair trial must be held _____ .

   a. publicly   b. secretly   c. without a jury

5. Most of the work of the C.I.A. is done _____ .

   a. in secret   b. in public   c. with Congress

6. During a state emergency, the government can call up soldiers from the _____ .

   a. Navy   b. Marines   c. National Guard

7. A nation with an absolute monarchy is _____ .

   a. Sweden   b. Saudi Arabia   c. Great Britain

8. In a socialist economy, the government provides many kinds of welfare benefits to _____ .

   a. all citizens   b. the elderly   c. the poor

9. One example of an alliance between the United States and other nations is _____ .

   a. N.A.T.O.   b. the Peace Corps   c. the I.N.F. Treaty

10. Only the _____ of the United Nations can decide to use military force or economic sanctions against other nations.

   a. Security Council   b. General Assembly   c. Trusteeship Council

Final Review

Write one or more sentences to answer each question.

1. What is representative government? _____

   _____

2. Why did the thirteen colonies become angry with King George? _____

   _____

3. What are two reasons that the Framers met to change and improve the Articles of

   Confederation? _____

   _____

4. List six ideas that the Framers agreed should be part of the Constitution. _____

   _____

   _____

5. Give an example of checks and balances. _____

   _____

6. Why is a census taken every ten years, and how does it affect government? _____

   _____

7. What are five powers of the President? _____

   _____

8. What is the power of judicial review? _____

   _____

9. What are two things Congress can do if the President vetoes a bill? _____

   _____

10. Why have many states rewritten their constitutions? _____

    _____

11. Why do states create local governments? _____

    _____

Name _____

12. What are the steps to being elected President, from nomination to election day?

_____

_____

13. What are three things that candidates spend money on during campaigns? _____

_____

14. What are two ways that citizens can influence government? _____

_____

15. How is the federal budget made? _____

_____

16. What are two ways the rights of an accused person are protected? _____

_____

_____

17. What are two ways that the national security is protected? _____

_____

_____

18. Explain the difference between a constitutional monarchy and an absolute

monarchy. _____

_____

19. Why is there interdependence between the United States and other nations? _____

_____

_____

20. What are three methods the United States uses to carry out its foreign policy? _____

_____

_____

Name _____

Final Test

Draw a circle around the letter of the correct answer.

1. The Framers of the Constitution used ideas about representative government from _____ to plan the Constitution.

   a. Great Britain and Rome
   b. France and Greece
   c. Rome and Greece

2. In the _____ , Thomas Jefferson told the world that the colonies wanted to become a free nation.

   a. Declaration of Independence
   b. Articles of Confederation
   c. Constitution

3. A system of government in which power is divided between a central government and state governments is called _____ .

   a. a democracy
   b. federalism
   c. the executive branch

4. The Three-Fifths Compromise was made about _____ .

   a. slavery
   b. senators
   c. federalism

5. The Constitution is the supreme _____ of the nation.

   a. democracy
   b. law
   c. idea

6. The Constitution can be changed by adding _____ .

   a. amendments
   b. a Preamble
   c. clauses

7. Freedom of religion, freedom of speech, and the right to a fair trial are guaranteed by the _____ .

   a. Declaration of Independence
   b. Articles of Confederation
   c. Bill of Rights

8. The Nineteenth Amendment gave _____ the right to vote.

   a. 18-year-olds
   b. women
   c. all people

9. The power of each branch of government is limited through _____ .

   a. compromises
   b. checks and balances
   c. amendments

10. Congress is made up of the House of Representatives and the _____ .

   a. presidency
   b. judicial branch
   c. Senate

11. Congress _____ when all business has been finished.

    a. votes   b. adjourns   c. compromises

12. The most important job of Congress is to _____ .

    a. control copyrights   b. approve treaties   c. make laws

13. The _____ branch carries out the laws of Congress.

    a. executive   b. legislative   c. judicial

14. The President cannot _____ .

    a. veto bills   b. make treaties   c. declare war

15. The _____ branch of government decides whether the actions of the President or the laws of Congress are unconstitutional.

    a. legislative   b. executive   c. judicial

16. Supreme Court justices are appointed by the _____ .

    a. Speaker of the House   b. Secretary of Justice   c. President

17. If the President _____ a bill, he can veto it.

    a. likes   b. opposes   c. overrides

18. Congress can override the President's veto of a bill with a _____ vote in both houses.

    a. two-thirds   b. three-fourths   c. majority

19. Bills are often killed in _____ .

    a. committee   b. the Senate   c. voting

20. The House and the Senate form a compromise bill in a _____ .

    a. subcommittee   b. political action   c. conference committee
                               committee

21. The Supreme Court uses _____ to decide whether a law is constitutional.

    a. judicial review   b. civil rights   c. appeals

22. Both state and federal governments have the power to _____ .

    a. pass marriage laws   b. collect taxes   c. create public school
                                              systems

23. Laws made by state legislatures are carried out by state _____ .

    a. agencies   b. committees   c. judges

24. One power that does not belong to the state governments is to _____ .

    a. establish local   b. coin money   c. pass traffic safety laws
        governments

25. Two ways for citizens to be involved in the state lawmaking process are through _____ .

    a. initiatives   b. appeals   c. sentences
        and referendums   and appointments   and convictions

26. One example of a service provided by local governments is _____ .

    a. social security   b. public libraries   c. military defense

27. The plan of action of a political party is called its _____ .

    a. platform   b. budget   c. document

28. To help voters learn the differences between the candidates on important issues, _____ are held before many elections.

    a. filibusters   b. conventions   c. debates

29. Interest groups form _____ to help political candidates win elections.

    a. PACs   b. political parties   c. lobbies

30. A presidential candidate for each party is chosen at the _____ .

    a. primary election   b. state convention   c. national convention

31. In the United States, the power of the military is limited by _____ leadership.

    a. medical   b. police   c. civilian

32. The government of Saudi Arabia is _____ .

    a. a constitutional   b. an absolute monarchy   c. a democracy
        monarchy

33. Examples of nations with parliamentary democracy are _____ .

    a. Sweden and   b. the United States   c. China and Saudi Arabia
        Great Britain   and Mexico

34. The Department of _____ is responsible for both foreign policy and the United States' ambassadors and embassies in other nations.

    a. Defense   b. Justice   c. State